BEST FRIENDS

BEST FRIENDS

The Ordinary Relationships

of Extraordinary People

GEORGE & KAREN GRANT

Cumberland House

NASHVILLE, TENNESSEE

Published by Cumberland House Publishing, Inc., 431 Harding Industrial Drive, Nashville, Tennessee 37211.

Jacket design by Tonya Presley
Text design by Bruce Gore, Gore Studios, Inc.

Library of Congress Cataloging-in-Publication Data

Grant, George, 1954–
    Best friends : the ordinary relationships of ordinary people / George & Karen Grant.
        p.   cm.
    ISBN 1-888952-71-7 (pbk. : alk. paper)
    1. Friendship—Case studies.   2. Friendship—Quotations, maxims, etc.   I. Grant, Karen
B., 1955–   II. Title.
BF575.F66G73   1998
177'.62—dc21   98-19817
                                                                          CIP

Printed in the United States of America
2 3 4 5 6 7 8 — 01 00 99 98

To the
Martins, Smiths, and Mansfields
Friends Indeed

And to the
Hunts, Thompsons, and Clarks
Friends In Deed

CONTENTS

Acknowledgments 9

Introduction 11

Comfort 17

CHRISTOPHER COLUMBUS AND FRA ANTONIO 21

Completeness 37

GEORGE WHITEFIELD AND BENJAMIN FRANKLIN 50

Diligence 61

ALEXANDER STEPHENS AND ABRAHAM LINCOLN 70

Discernment 79

TEDDY ROOSEVELT AND HENRY CABOT LODGE 90

Duty 101

ELIZABETH AND JOHN BUNYAN 110

Forbearance 119

JOHN BUCHAN AND THOMAS NELSON 129

Joy 139

MONICA AND AUGUSTINE 148

Kindness 155

GEORGE WASHINGTON AND THOMAS MIFFLIN 165

Remembrance 175

BROTHER BRYAN AND LESLIE KETTERING 182

ACKNOWLEDGMENTS

"Tell me what company thou keepest,
and I'll tell thee what thou art."
MIGUEL DE CERVANTES

It should be little surprise to anyone that this book about friends would not have been possible apart from the gracious ministrations of many friends. Not only did they encourage us along the way as this project slowly took shape, they modeled before us its most basic principles and provided its necessary inspirations.

We have been blessed by a prodigious number of enduring friendships. Gene and Susan Hunt, Anthony and Sharon Gordon, Tom and Jody Clark, Jim and Gwen Smith, Steve and Marijean Green, Mark and Barbara Thompson, Stephen and Trish Mansfield, Don and Suzanne Martin, Steve and Wendy Wilkins, Phil and Sally Bartels, and Tom and Yo Clark are all gratefully accounted among that number. They are evidence that despite our all too obvious faults, we have had the privilege of keeping very good company indeed. We are what we are because of them. And we write what we write thanks to them.

Ron and Julie Pitkin offered enthusiastic support for this project from its early gestation, and they endured its long and frequent delays with remarkable forbearance. We are grateful for their abiding in friendship and their vision for publishing excellence.

The soundtrack for this project was provided by Steve Green, Loreena McKennitt, William Coulter, and Shelley Phillips, while the midnight musings were provided by Paul Johnson, Dorothy Sayers, Jeremiah Burroughs, and G.K. Chesterton.

To all these, we offer our sincerest thanks.

Of course, our deepest debt in life is owed to our three beloved children, Joel, Joanna, and Jesse. They have been our dearest, surest, and best friends. It should come as no surprise then that they were our chief inspiration for this collection of quotations and stories.

LENTENTIDE 1998
King's Meadow Farm

INTRODUCTION

"There is a friend that sticketh closer than a brother."
KING SOLOMON

According to the old adage, "Behind every great man stands a great woman." While that truism may well be true, it might just as easily be asserted, "Behind every great man—or, for that matter, behind every great woman—stands a great friend." Indeed, friendship is one of the most powerful, though underrated, forces in shaping the destinies of men and nations.

If love is what makes the world go round, friendship is what keeps it on its axis. If romance is life's most delectable delight, friendship is its most essential staple. If affectionate intimacy is its sweet dessert, enduring companionship is its meat and potatoes.

Though history is generally recorded as a series of individual achievements or corporate movements, more often than not momentous events are shaped by the hidden persuasions of interpersonal concerns. They are the first fruits of familiarity.

Friendship affords us the support, cooperation, and accountability necessary to accomplish the varied tasks before us. It lends us the camaraderie, succor, and fellowship necessary to endure inevitable hardships. It offers us the nurturing, discipling, and mentoring necessary to succeed in the face of great obstacles.

The annals of time offer clear testimony to the important role friends have played in keeping great men and women on track in times of discouragement, defeat, or despair. Quietly, beyond the public eye, out of the limelight they prodded, encouraged, chided, enlightened, motivated, impelled, and influenced. So while the marvelous achievements they provoked are chalked up solely to their comrades—to such men as Washington, Lincoln, and Roosevelt—to a very great extent, those unheralded friends were really no less responsible. The constancy, candor, and counsel of the true friend is the stuff of which triumph is ultimately made.

This book is an exploration of that phenomenon. It examines the role friendship has played in the lives of some of the most remarkable men and women of all time.

Of course, not all friendships were created equal. Different friendships have distinctly different characteristics. Some are the happily predicable result of like attracting like—the communion of shared interests, experiences, and concerns. Others are the most unlikely pairings of opposites—the attraction of oddly complementary contrasts.

Some friendships last over the long course of a lifetime. Others are but for a single season. Some are able to withstand the separations of time and distance. Others are the surprising fruit of convenience and proximity. But all leave their unique impress.

This book then is a profile of several subtle varieties of friendship that have shaped some of the most notable lives and careers in history—each offering an insightful perspective into the dynamics of human achievement.

Thus, the adversarial relationship of Abraham Lincoln and Alexander Stephens is as stimulating as the filial relationship of Theodore Roosevelt and Henry Cabot Lodge. The marital relationship of John and Elizabeth Bunyan is as revealing as the pastoral relationship of Christopher Columbus and Fra Antonio de Marchena. Notice, that we did not choose to profile some of the more famous friendships in history—that of Napoleon and Josephine, of Thomas Jefferson and John Adams, of Percy Shelley and Lord Byron, of Winston Churchill and Franklin Roosevelt, of C.S. Lewis and J.R.R. Tolkien, or of G.K. Chesterton and Hilaire Belloc. Instead, we have chose the rather more historically obscure friendships believing that they more dramatically illustrate the varied profundities of abiding relations and their impact upon the destinies of men and nations. Our object, after all, has been to explore the ordinary relationships of extraordinary people.

At a time when the hurly-burly of modern life has squeezed most of our relationships into the rude mold of hurried encounters, shallow exchanges, and unrealistic expectations it is especially therapeutic for us to revisit the manner and the means of authentic friendship—so that we might once again know its bolstering trust, security, and comfort.

Thus, *Best Friends: The Ordinary Relationships of Extraordinary People* includes a wide-ranging anthology of short quotations from correspondence, publications, epigrams, vignettes, anecdotes, and conversations that highlight the peculiar characteristics of different friendships as well as brief biographical profiles of nine singular relationships—thus moving from the general to the particular.

According to the great Victorian pulpiteer, Charles Haddon Spurgeon, "Friendship is one of the sweetest joys of life. Many might have failed beneath the bitterness of their trail had they not found a friend." It is our sincerest hope and prayer that this collection of snippets and insights may heighten your awareness of the great treasure you have in your own friendships—and that such an awareness will encourage you to do all that you are called to do and be all that you are called to be.

BEST FRIENDS

Comfort

There is no greater solace in times of trouble than the concern of a friend. Somehow they can comfort us without the easy resort to cliches, maxims, bromides, or hackneyed stereotypes—often even without words. They know us. They understand us. They care for us. All too often the great men and women through the ages were able to achieve what they did only because they had the recourse of friendship in times of adversity.

And I will gladly share with you your pain,
If it turn out I can no comfort bring;
For tis a friend's right, please let me explain,
To share in woeful as in joyful things.
Geoffrey Chaucer, 1343-1400

"Real friendship is shown in times of trouble;
prosperity is full of friends."
Abraham Kuyper, 1837-1920

Comfort

"A friend loves at all times and a brother is born for adversity"

King Solomon, Proverbs 17:17

"Misfortune tests the sincerity of friends."

Robert E. Lee, 1807-1870

"Best friend, my wellspring in the wilderness."

George Eliot, 1819-1890

Love is like the wild rose-briar;
Friendship like the holly-tree.
The holly is dark when the rose-briar blooms,
But which will bloom most constantly?

Emily Bronte, 1818-1848

Comfort.

CHRISTOPHER COLUMBUS, 1451–1506
AND FRA ANTONIO DE MARCHENA, 1460–1521

By all accounts the innovative navigator and explorer from the Italian Renaissance city of Genoa, Christopher Columbus, was universal in his interests and moderate in his opinions—unlike most modern men who are moderate in their interests and universal in their opinions. He was an interesting man in what most matters because he was a man interested in most matters.

Though he had no formal schooling, as a youngster he knew a great deal of classical literature by heart long before he could really get it into his head. Early on he knew whole passages of Thucidides, Plutarch, Augustine, and Jerome without a notion of the meaning of most of it—which is perhaps the best way to begin to appreciate the classics.

The son of a weaver, trader, and merchant, he first went to sea when he was about ten. Besides helping at home with the woolens, he began to venture out on short sailing excursions to Portofino to load dry fish, to Savona with bolts of his father's cloth, or to Corsica to sell Genoese dry goods in the festival markets.

Like so many of Genoa's progeny, he was immediately smitten by the romance and grandeur of the sea. He was cheerfully constrained by its ironies and contradictions. He loved the great angry roaring waves that tossed ships like the chiefs of charging clans; he loved the drifting stillness beyond breakwater that cast vessels gliding on moon-whitened calm. He reveled in the wild romance of strenuous labor, of blistered palms, of skin as tough as tree bark, and strained muscles like the sinews of Signorelli devils; he reveled in the tender romance of lolling at the tiller while the skipper retreated below and the mate snoozed on the sunny side of the deck. He inhaled the robust expansiveness of the briny breeze; he exhaled the vigorous closeness of the dense hold. He flourished in the camaraderie of the crew with an insubordinate glee; he flourished in the solitude of months away from home with a fond grace. He put his trust in the wind and God's providence; he left nothing to chance and honed his nautical skills to razor sharpness. His craft was mystical; his craft was scientific. His passions were stubborn; his passions were sound. In short, his infatuation with sailing was as fierce and unequivocal, and as gentle and mysterious, as the sea itself.

Over the next seven or eight years he sailed whenever he could. Apparently he was a quick study and never wanted for opportunities to sail. His keen powers of observation, his sharp wits, his appetite for learning, his vast intellect, and his innate sense of direction all served him extremely well. By the time he was eighteen he knew the western Mediterranean like the pocket of a familiar cloak—and he abandoned the weaver's loom for a life at sea.

He was successful enough as a sailor to ultimately relocate to what was then the unrivaled seafaring center of the world, the little realm of Portugal. It daily sent adventurers, cartographers, merchants, astronomers, missionaries, navigators, settlers, cosmographers, and explorers out into the unknown. Representatives of the crown skirted eastward along the Guinea coastline. They riposted westward toward Ultima Thule. They probed the waters beyond the Azores in the north and the Cape Verdes in the south. They carved out new routes to the Baltics and reclaimed old ones in the Mediterranean. They were unchallenged as the masters of the seas. Clearly, it was the place to be at the end of the fifteenth century.

Columbus was not only dazzled by the queer sights and sounds of the land's piratical romance with commerce, he was dazed by the mysterious humors of its intellectual romance with books. He read voraciously. He collected works by his favorite authors. And he studied new ideas with an academic intensity uncommon outside the cloister.

His superior grasp of the navigator's art—combined with his wide learning and refinement—enabled him to establish himself as a highly sought after fleet captain. His prosperous enterprises eventually enabled him to settle with his young family on Portugal's colonial island paradise of Porto Santo. He was now free to pursue his wide-ranging intellectual and scientific interests—interrupted only by an occasional commercial sailing commission.

He was already well versed in the most prominent works of Marinus, Strabo, Ctesias, Onesicritus, Nearchus, Pliny, and Alfragano. So, he began to explore farther afield with the physical and philosophical theorems of Plato, Averroes, Solinus, d'Ailly, Savanarolla, and Capitolinus. He was particularly captivated by the calculations of Mandeville, the prophesies of Seneca, the geographies of Ptolemy, and the narratives of Marco Polo.

As he read and studied, an idea began to take shape in his mind—or rather an appetite began to stir in his gullet. He began to wonder if it might not be possible to circumnavigate the globe. He began to wonder if the expanse of the ocean could be crossed. He began to wonder if the impasse in the Middle East—the conquest of Eastern Christendom by the Moslems and the failure of the Crusades to liberate them—could not be overcome by some new and innovative means. He simply began to wonder—which is the most natural of responses to great literature.

Columbus began to gather evidence to support his hypothesis. He spoke with navigators and scholars. He inquired of clergymen and royalty. And he devoted untold hours to gazing out across the western horizon—he plotted the course of the currents, measured the force of the winds, and documented the changes in the seasons. He considered, conjectured, and compared. Ultimately, a plan began to take shape—he called it the Great Enterprise

Before long, the idea had begun to obsess and possess him. Thus, Columbus started the search for sponsors. He fully expected that it would be a short search. As it turned out though, it would be an agonizingly long journey through the dark night of his own soul.

Columbus first took his idea to the dynamic regent of Portugal, Joao II. The king found the Genoese navigator to be bluff and chatty, urgent and affectionate, precise and hortatory. He had never met anyone who was so altogether complex: wise and fierce, calculating and inspired, passionate and intelligent, exacting and sharply judging, and endlessly, charitably, imaginatively curious about all sorts of small and obscene, trivial and terrible, glorious and profane human dilemmas. Thus, he was as much attracted to the idea of the Discoverer as he was to the Discoverer's idea.

He was immediately inclined to accept the proposal Columbus had laid before him. But so as not to make a hasty emotional decision, the king referred the matter to his most trusted maritime advisory commissioners—a circle of counselors he had only recently appointed to deal with such things. The Junta dos Mathematicos, was composed of renowned experts in both science and theology—men well-suited to consider the technical aspects of any nautical proposal.

After deliberating for some eighteen months, the commissioners determined that Columbus was fancifully optimistic in his calculations. The question of the sphericity of the earth was not a concern to them—as many modern historians would lead us to believe. All educated men had known the planet was round since early antiquity. Instead, the commissioners doubted the estimate of the circumference of the globe that Columbus had computed. They questioned his identification and analysis of the trade winds. They remained dubious in the face of hearsay physical clues. They were skeptical about his navigational experience and skill. And they remained unconvinced of the expedition's practical benefits to the crown. In the process, they dismissed the mass of his accumulated evidence—perhaps they knew that it would have irreparably harmed the topography of their misunderstanding of him. Like so many modern men have—or rather, like the ideologues of all ages have—they turned facts which destroyed their theories into exceptions which proved their rules.

All too frequently, history appears to recant—it abandons the patterns of our carefully plotted logic.

Besides the technical concerns of the commission, there were at least three other reasons why Joao decided to pass on the opportunity to finance the western passage: first, he had already committed enormous resources into an effort to reach the Indies by circumnavigating the continent of Africa; second, the demands of Columbus—that he be admitted to the royal roster, that he be appointed Grand Admiral, that he be named perpetual viceroy of all discovered territories, that he be allowed to lead a resultant Crusade to liberate Jerusalem, and that he be given a full tenth of any accrued profits—seemed overly exorbitant; and third, other mariners were anxious to undertake a clandestine exploration to steal the Genoese transplant's strategy at far less cost to the crown.

Whatever the reasons, the Portuguese rejection was a stunning blow to Columbus. He was so completely convinced that his plan was the will of God that he had a hard time imagining how or why anyone would question its validity. In his mind it was as preordained as salvation. His confidence was shattered.

And as if that were not enough for him to have to deal with, a few days later, his beloved wife, Felipa, died suddenly. Now his whole world was shattered.

Discouraged, despondent, and broken hearted, Columbus gained passage on a ship and secretly sailed with his young son to Palos—an Andalusian port under the control of Isabella of Castile.

Upon arriving at Palos, Columbus and Diego went immediately to La Rabida—a small church annexed to a Franciscan friary. There they worshiped—as was the Navigator's habit following any voyage—and gave thanks. Afterward, Columbus intended to cross the Rio Tinto and proceed to the nearby town of Huelva where he hoped to be able to stay in the home of Violante Moniz Perestrello—his sister-in-law. But once again, providence intervened.

At La Rabida, Columbus met Fra Antonio de Marchena—a Franciscan friar who was not only a cleric of great piety and reputation but a scientist who had gained repute as a fine astronomer. The two men became fast friends, and Columbus was persuaded to enjoy the hospitality of the Minorite manor for the next several weeks. In fact, La Rabida would be the closest thing to a permanent home that he and his son would have for the rest of his life.

He quickly discovered that he shared a number of keen interests with the friar. Both were widely read. Both were conversant on the current state of cartographical and cosmographical thought. Both were skilled rhetoriticians. Both yearned passionately for the revival of the crusading spirit to drive the Saracens out of the occupied lands of Christendom—and the consequent liberation of the Holy

Sepulchre out of Saracen hands. Both were pious but inquisitive theologically. And both loved the challenge of adventure.

Columbus apparently gushed a Niagara of information about his conception of a western route to the Indies—and Fra Antonio immediately grasped its significance. It was not long before he completely shared the enthusiasm of Columbus for the Great Enterprise.

Over the next few years, the friar would become the Discoverer's greatest advocate. He encouraged the further refinement of the Grand Design. He introduced him at court. He upheld him during his difficulties. He looked to the care and education of Diego. He lent him spiritual counsel and support. But most significantly, at a time when most of the relationships of Columbus were as flat as shadows and as superficial as diagrams, the friar offered him genuine friendship.

He also offered him books.

The library in the cloisters of La Rabida was an undoubted feast for the senses. Adjacent to the abandoned scriptorium, it was immediately impressive though not at all imposing. It had seven walls and was surmounted by the sort of high round-headed arch that shamelessly borrowed from a Moorish vocabulary. One of the walls was pierced by a narrow passageway flanked by two unadorned rosewood columns. Against each of the other walls stood huge oaken cases, laden with books neatly arranged. Each case bore a scroll with a number, and so did each individual shelf—obviously corresponding to some sort of arcane cataloging system. In the center of the room was a long low table, also laden with books.

To the frustrated and discouraged Columbus, that library, to which he was given full access by Fra Antionio, was an earthly elysium. It seemed to represent everything that he aspired to and it embodied everything that he yearned for. It was a sort of nexus of piety and sensuality, of holiness and seduction. He imagined that it was the cenacle of virtue, the vessel of erudition, the ark of prudence, the tower of wisdom, the domain of meekness, the bastion of strength, and the thurible of sanctity as well as the crucible of dissipation, the throne room of desire, the caryatid of opulence, the repository of salaciousness, the milieu of concupiscence, and the truss of extravagance.

The rich fragrance of hand-oiled Moroccan leathers, the visual panoply of deep natural hues, the effluvium of fine vellum, the hollow ring of sequestered silence, the sacred spectacle of light filtered through rose windows, and the hush of monkish thoughtfulness combined to grant the room an air of amplitude. The total effect was of a concert of alluring terrestrial beauty and majestic supernatural signals.

Fra Antonio taught him that the creative arts consisted of signs. Thus, if images were, as Aristotle asserted, "the literature of the layman," then books consisted of signs of signs. And libraries consisted of signs of signs of signs. They were thus, the truest of all the creative arts—combining rhythm, tone, structure, progression, logic, melody, heft, texture, redolence, cipher, perspective, harmony, balance, epic, symbol, emblem, saga, craftsmanship, hue, lyric, form, function, ballad, and sanctity. They were united in their variety and varied in their unity, unique in their diversity and diverse in their apt assembly. They were sustained by a law at once heavenly and worldly.

In short, the hungry scientific mind of Columbus was invested with a new creative imagination by his friend and mentor. As a result, he began to revisit the classic natural history texts of antiquity in a whole new light—and as a result, he made a startling discovery: the wisdom of many of the ancients actually reinforced his basic ideas. There pass, from time to time, over the minds of men certain

vast and mighty moods which make the movements of the world.
Such was the mood that drove Columbus into the library at La
Rabida and into the care of his friend Fra Antonio. In some ways, his
experience there was more obtusely symbolic than it was acutely evi-
dential—as is often the case when mere men must deal in signs of
signs. Even so, the case for the Great Enterprise seemed more compelling to him with every passing day.

With Fra Antonio's referral and recommendation in hand,
Columbus was able to approach Don Enrique de Guzman—the fab-
ulously wealthy Duke of Medina—with the idea for the transoceanic
voyage. The duke was apparently very interested—so much so that
he actually promised to equip a fleet for Columbus. But as fate
would have it, a political squabble ended their discussions prema-
turely and they were never resumed.

Next Columbus turned to Don Luis de la Cerda—the industrious
Count of Medina Celi. Again, the Discoverer met with an quick pos-
itive response. The count—who owned a merchant fleet—enthusias-
tically pledged his willingness to underwrite the entire venture. But
before he could outfit the necessary caravels he had to secure royal
permission. So, application was made of the Castilian queen.

That would be the first Isabella had heard of the Great
Enterprise. She was intrigued. She was intrigued by the comprehen-
sive plan that Columbus had prepared. And she was intrigued by
Columbus himself—his quick-witted and long-winded demeanor
was a far cry from the condescending courtiers that normally sur-
rounded her.

Isabella was so intrigued in fact, that she denied the count permission to proceed with his investment. Instead she submitted the
idea of the western crossing to her own advisory commission.

For the next seven years Columbus lived his life as an uninter-
rupted series of preludes. He waited for the maddeningly slow
wheels of government to turn. Though he was placed on the royal
payroll, became a social fixture at the court, and was regularly enter-
tained at the magnificent estates of princes, dukes, and lords, those
years of waiting were the worst in his life. He was a man of action.
He was meant for the open seas, not the turbulent waters of political
intrigue. He was impatient with bureaucracy. In fact, he came to
believe that it was a curse-like repetition and indigestion. It was only
the constancy, encouragement, and friendship of Fra Antonio that
kept him going in those long difficult years.

When the Moors of Granada finally surrendered to the Christian host on January 2, 1492, Columbus had the joy of marching in the victory procession. With every obstacle out of the way, it seemed certain that he would soon be summoned before the queen to receive final instructions for his Great Enterprise. And indeed he was. But to his utter dismay she simply rejected the project out of hand.

After nearly seven years of frustration, the Castilian ordeal appeared to be over. Columbus packed to leave the Iberian realms—for where, he did not yet know.

But at that point, his friend Fra Antonio—now the head of the friary at La Rabida—intervened for Columbus at the court in one final titanic effort. The powerful Luis de Santangel—King Ferdinand's keeper of the privy purse and treasurer of the Santa Hermandad—did the same in Aragon. And somehow, someway, and for some unknown reason, the monarchs of the two matrimonial realms reversed themselves.

A royal messenger found the dejected Columbus walking toward the village of Pinos-Puente, somewhere between Granada and Santa Fe. He accepted the summons to return to the court without a moment's hesitation.

And the rest of the story is, as they say, history.

By the end of summer, Columbus was prodding the Nina, the Pinta, and the Santa Maria westward toward destiny under Isabella's crest and Ferdinand's pinion. The Great Enterprise was made possible, in more ways than one, by the ordinary friendship of two extraordinary men.

Completeness

*W*ithout friends we all remain rather unbalanced.
*Friendship enables us to tie off the loose ends of our experience,
to straighten the rumpled corners of our personality, to darn
the frayed gaps in our expression, and to hem the edges of our
interest. Friendship makes us better because friendship makes
us whole. No man is an island—or to the extent that he is,
he suffers. Wise men and women have always
known this only too well.*

"But because our expression is imperfect we need friendship to fill up the imperfections. A man of our own type or tastes will understand our meaning before it is expressed; certainly a long time before it is perfectly expressed."

G.K. Chesterton, 1874-1936

"No man is the whole of himself. His friends are the rest of him."

George Whitefield, 1714-1770

"He is your friend who pushes you nearer to God."

Abraham Kuyper, 1837-1920

"No man has learned to live until he can rise above the narrow confines of his individualistic concerns to the broader concerns of all humanity. Length without breadth is like a self contained tributary having no outward flow to the ocean. Stagnant, still, and stale it lacks both life and freshness. In order to live creatively and meaningfully, our self-concern must be wedded to other concerns."

Martin Luther King Jr., 1929-1968

"To be capable of steady friendship or lasting love, are the two greatest proofs, not only of goodness of heart, but of strength of mind."

William Hazlitt, 1778-1830

"All kinds of things rejoiced my soul in the company of my friends—to talk and laugh and do each other kindnesses; read pleasant books together, pass from lightest jesting to talk of the deepest things and back again; differ without rancour, as a man might differ with himself, and when most rarely dissension arose find our normal agreement all the sweeter for it; teach each other or learn from each other; be impatient for the return of the absent, and welcome them with joy on their homecoming; these and such like things, proceeding from our hearts as we gave affection and received it back, and shown by face, by voice, by the eyes, and a thousand other pleasing ways, kindled a flame which infused our very souls and of many made us one. This is what men value in friends."

St. Augustine, 354-430

"Though love be deeper, yet friendship is more wide."

*{ *Arthur Quiller-Couch, 1863-1944* }*

A true friend is a pearl
Your deepest needs
And so spares you the shame
Of giving your heart
And its hidden desires a name.

*{ *A.A. Milne, 1882-1956* }*

"Those friends thou hast, and their adoption tried, grapple them to thy soul with hoops of steel."
❧ Hamlet, *William Shakespeare, c. 1564-1616* ❧

"Friendship is unnecessary, like philosophy, like art. It has no survival value; rather it is one of those things that give value to survival."
❧ *C.S. Lewis, 1898-1963* ❧

"A faithful friend is the medicine of life."
❧ *Quohelleth, Ecclesiasticus 6:16* ❧

"A friend is a present you give yourself."
Robert Louis Stevenson, 1850-1894

"A father is a treasure; a brother is a comfort; a friend is both."
Benjamin Franklin, 1706-1790

"When two go together, one of them at least looks forward to see what is best; a man by himself, though he be careful, still has less mind in him than two, and his wits have less weight."
Homer, c. 900 B.C.

Our true friends will stretch us intellectually, will understand our deepest longings and fondest dreams, and will encourage us to embrace the future in dynamic and constructive ways. In difficult times they are most assuredly there for us—and we are there for them—physically, emotionally, and spiritually. Likewise, in times of blessing our fellowship is sweet, sure, and secure. Indeed, our true friends are our soul-mates—those whom we can love and trust so implicitly that we are actually able to think out loud in their welcome presence. We are able to talk with them, listen with them, and share long comfortable silences with them. Oh what glorious joy our true friends are to us.

John Buchan, 1875-1940

Friendship is a pledge that covers varying degrees of strength and intensity and is as universal as the smile. We need all kinds of friends—neighbors, high school buddies, work mates, and spouses alike. Whether we swap theories on child rearing over a cup of coffee, or just good mystery novels, all friends offer us the invitation to be ourselves. Not everyone has the capacity to become your best friend, even though you share with them a special part of you. Best friends reach a higher level—it is a meeting of minds, a bound loyalty. A best friend is the person you want to go to first with good news—or bad. As soul mates, best friends can practically speak with their eyes—just a knowing glance speaks a thousand words. The common ground is endless.

John Sage, 1902-1987

He speaketh not;
And yet there lies
A conversation
In his eyes.

Henry Wadsworth Longfellow, 1807-1882

Hand grasps at hand,
Eye lights eye in good friendship
And great hearts expand
And grow one
In the sense of this world's life.

Ralph Waldo Emerson, 1803-1882

"A friend hears the song of the heart and sings it when memory fails."
Martin Luther, 1483-1546

"As we have private ties, so we should have public ties. As we have private prayers, so we should have public prayers. As we have private houses, so we should have public houses."
G.K. Chesterton, 1874-1936

"Tell me what company thou keepest, and I'll tell thee what thou art."
Miguel de Cervantes, 1547-1616

"A friend is someone you can call in the middle of the night when panic over your new job suddenly sets in, or when the dullness of your old job finally becomes unbearable, or when your diet has just brushed aside by a late night binge, or your bald spot has at last brushed aside your few remaining filaments of dignity—or even when you just need to prove to yourself there is someone you can call in the middle of the night."

Tristan Gylberd, 1954-

"Friendship can take different turns—it can run like a river, quietly and sustainingly through life; it can erupt like a geyser, forcefully and intermittently at times; or it can explode like a meteor, altering the atmosphere so that nothing ever looks, feels, or functions the same again."

Ansel Adams, 1902-1984

"I don't think any woman in power really has a happy life unless she's got a large number of women friends—because you sometimes must go and sit down and let down your hair with someone you can trust totally."

Margaret Thatcher, 1925-

GEORGE WHITEFIELD, 1714-1770
AND BENJAMIN FRANKLIN, 1706-1790

He was America's first celebrity. Though just twenty-five years old
when he began touring the sparsely settled colonies in 1738, George
Whitefield was an immediate sensation. And he remained so for the
rest of his life. Over the next thirty years, amidst some seven visits
from his native England, he would leave his mark on the lives of virtually every English-speaking soul living on this side of the
Atlantic—from the cosmopolitan businessmen of Philadelphia and
the seasoned traders of Boston to the yeomen farmers of Virginia
and the frontier adventurers of Canada.

Perhaps it is surprising to us that an evangelist would be the most
outstanding man of that day—a day graced by the likes of so many
great men: Peyton Randolph, Samuel Adams, Patrick Henry, John
Hancock, Alexander Hamilton, John Jay, George Mason
Gouverneur Morris, Charles Pickney, Edmund Randolph, James
Madison, and George Washington. But it was no surprise to them.

Whitefield literally took America by storm. "When he arrived in
the colonies," says historian Mark Noll, "he was simply an event."

Wherever he went, vast crowds gathered to hear him. Commerce would cease. Shops would close. Farmers would leave their plows mid-furrow. And affairs of the greatest import would be postponed. One of his sermons in the Boston Common actually drew more listeners than the city's entire population. Another in Philadelphia spilled over onto more than a dozen city blocks. Still another in Savannah recorded the largest single crowd ever to gather anywhere in the colonies—despite the scant local population.

Some said he blazed across the public firmament like a "heavenly comet." Some said he was a "magnificent fascination of the like heretofore unknown." Others said he "startled the world awake like a bolt from the blue." There can be little doubt that he lived up to his reputation as the "marvel of the age." As historian Harry Stout has written: "He was a preacher capable of commanding mass audiences—and offerings—across two continents, without any institutional support, through the sheer power of his personality. Whitefield wrote best-selling journals and drew audiences totaling in the millions. White and black, male and female, friends and enemies—all flocked in unprecedented numbers to hear the Grand Itinerant. Whenever he visited, people could do anything, it seemed, but stay away."

By all accounts, he was the "father of modern evangelism." He sparked a deeply effecting revival of portentous proportions—the Great Awakening. He helped to pioneer one of the most enduring church reform movements in history—Methodism. And he laid the foundations for perhaps the greatest experiment in liberty the world has yet known—the American Republic.

All the greatest men of the day were in unabashed awe of his oratorical prowess. Shakespearean actor David Garrick said, "I would give a hundred guineas if I could say *oh* like Mr. Whitefield." John Witherspoon declared, "No creature of God has ever been endowed with such resources for the eternal persuasion of men and nations." And Sarah Edwards—the astute and unaffected wife of the dean of American theologians, Jonathan Edwards—remarked, "He is a born orator."

But he was equally beloved for his righteous character. George Washington said, "Upon his lips the Gospel appears even to the coarsest of men as sweet and as true as, in fact, it is." Patrick Henry mused, "Would that every bearer of God's glad tidings be as fit a vessel of grace as Mr. Whitefield." And the poet, John Greenleaf Whittier wrote of him:

That life of pure intent,
That voice of warning, yet eloquent,
Of one on the errands of angels sent.

Yet despite his wide acclaim and popularity, Whitefield was often ridiculed, scorned, and persecuted for his faith and work. Hecklers blew trumpets and shouted obscenities at him as he preached. Enraged mobs often attacked his meetings, robbing, beating, and humiliating his followers. Men were maimed. Women were stripped and occasionally raped. Whitefield himself was subjected to unimaginable brutality—he was clubbed twice, stoned once, whipped at least half a dozen times, and beaten a half a dozen more. And he lived constantly under the pall of death threats. Once, he recorded in his journal: "I was honored with having a few stones, dirt, rotten eggs, and pieces of dead cats thrown at me. Nevertheless, the Lord was gracious, and a great number were awakened unto life."

Amazingly, it was not just the profane who condemned Whitefield's work. He was also opposed by the religious establishment. Accused of being a "fanatic," of being "intolerant," and of "fanning the flames" of "vile bigotry," he was often in "more danger of attack from the clergy than he was from the worldly."

As a result, biographer Arnold Dallimore says, "Whitefield's entire evangelistic life was an evidence of his physical courage." He fearlessly faced his opposition and continued his work. Though often stung by the vehemence of the opposition he faced, he refused to take it personally, attributing it rather to what he called the "offense of the Gospel."

His unlikely chief defender and best friend during those trying days was the renowned free-thinker and skeptic, Benjamin Franklin. The two had met shortly after the evangelist's first visit to Franklin's hometown, Philadelphia. Surprisingly, the two became fast friends.

Patriot, inventor, scientist, philosopher, musician, editor, printer and diplomat, Franklin brought the prestige of his unparalleled achievements to the public service that consumed over half of his life. He was the living example of the richness of life that man can achieve with the freedom—and the will—to do so. In many senses, he was the first American, and he was a Founding Father of the first rank. His rise from apprentice to man of affairs was paralleled by an ever-widening circle of interests. His curiosity led him from subject to subject: he mastered printing, learned French, invented a stove, discovered electrical principles, organized a postal service, and helped discover the Gulf Stream.

As a young man, Franklin had begun to question the pious assumptions of his neighbors. His wide-ranging intellect seemed to lead him in every direction except toward orthodoxy. He became a frank Deist—rejecting much of the Bible as mere moralistic aspiration or idealistic fantasy. Over the years he had become rather notorious for his reckless promiscuity, disrespectful cynicism, and esoteric inquiries. He was hardly a prime candidate to become an intimate and confidante of the "father of evangelicalism."

Nevertheless, Franklin was fascinated by Whitefield. He was stunned by the passion, conviction, and suasion of his preaching. He was intrigued by the intellectual honesty, theological consistency, and moral integrity of his work. He was inspired by the courage, tenacity, and selflessness of his personal life. And he was gripped by the sheer skill, beauty, and balance of his discipline.

He once said, "He can bring men to tears merely by pronouncing the word Mesopotamia." Another time he quipped, "Never go to one of Mr. Whitefield's assemblies with money in your pouch, or you shall surely soon find it empty—such is his alluring power over the will of his hearers." And again he said, "There is hardly another minister of the Gospel alive who can so bring to life the truth and relevancy of the Scriptures. Almost, he persuadeth me to believe." He was particularly taken by the fact that Whitefield was as delightful one-on-one as he was before his vast throngs. "He is a fine conversationalist and a sympathetic listener. He is an ideal friend."

But then, Franklin proved to be an ideal friend as well. He undertook the publication of Whitefield's journals and sermons. It was a good business decision—the books were instant best-sellers on both sides of the Atlantic. But it was also a boon to both of their personal lives. Over the course of nearly thirty years the two men carried on a vibrant correspondence and forged an intimate friendship that sustained them both throughout the rest of their lives. They encouraged one another. They stimulated one another. They inspired one another. They cajoled one another. And they comforted one another.

As his country's representative in England in the 1760s, Franklin defended America's position before hostile, arrogant officials; he helped win repeal of the Stamp Act and pleaded for American representation in Parliament. In the 1770s he continued to try to reason with British officials, but they were inflexible. Eventually, he returned to America, ready to support the cause of independence.

Whitefield meanwhile continued his evangelistic work—having turned over the fledgling Methodist movement in England to his ambitious disciple John Wesley. He was awakened to the fact that the eternal liberties inherent in Biblical grace had birthed in his American hearers a hunger for the temporal liberties inherent in Biblical law. He found himself giving counsel to the men who would in short order lead a revolution and launch a nation. The influence of Franklin's friendship had made his message more relevant than ever before.

Franklin made the connection between the message of the gospel and the message of freedom early on. He had learned from Whitefield the principle that "the Lordship of Christ touches every arena of life." Now he was encouraged to apply that principle to the emerging American republic. The influence of Whitefield's friendship had made his work more focused than ever before.

Just before Whitefield died—of exhaustion following a strenuous evangelistic campaign throughout the middle colonies—the two friends had exchanged letters regarding plans for a new Christian

settlement across the Appalachian Mountains in what is today
Tennessee. Whitefield was interested in seeing how the principles of
grace might be reflected in the temporal world. Franklin was interested in seeing how the reflections the eternal world might be prin-
cipled in freedom. Clearly, each had helped to transform the thinking of the other. As historian Douglas Southall Freeman has said,
"Their friendship was a living example of iron sharpening iron."

In the years afterward, the impact of their friendship continued
to manifest itself in a number of ways.

In the Continental Congress Franklin headed the committee
that organized the American postal system, helped draft the Articles
of Confederation, and began negotiations with the French for aid.
And he helped draft and signed the Declaration of Independence.
His fellow delegates were surprised by his sober attentiveness and
respectful virtue. It became evident that he was the colonies' best
choice as commissioner to France: well known as a scientist and
philosopher, he was warmly welcomed in Paris, and his position as a
world figure, coupled with his diplomatic skill, helped him negoti-
ate the alliance with France which brought America desperately
needed military support. Soon after, he began negotiating with the

British for peace, but only after the French fleet had joined with Washington to defeat Cornwallis at Yorktown, would the British consider granting independence. Franklin signed the peace treaty September 3, 1783.

After he returned to America, Franklin had one more vital role to play: at the Constitutional Convention his very presence gave weight and authority to the proceedings, and he used his influence to moderate conflicts. On at least two occasions, the famous skeptic called on the deadlocked delegates to pray. On another he recommended that the tense proceedings be "ameliorated by the attendance of a chaplain" and "by his regular ministrations." And on the final day he appealed to the delegates: "I confess that there are several parts of this Constitution which I do not at present approve, but I am not sure I shall never approve them. For having lived long, I have experienced many instances of being obliged by better information, or fuller consideration, to change opinions even on important subjects, which I once thought right, but found to be otherwise. I cannot help expressing a wish that every member of the Convention who may still have objections to it, would with me, on this occasion, doubt a little of his own infallibility, and to make manifest our unanimity, put his name on this instrument." A few minutes later all but three delegates signed the Constitution.

A friendship had helped to shape a culture—and then afterward, to make a nation.

Diligence

*Relationships require effort. Like a healthy marriage,
a solid friendship takes work. We must be vigilant. We must
be watchful. We must take care not to let the bonds of care to
suffer from either the suffocation of too much attention or the
degeneration of too little attention. Men and women of accomplishment have thus always taken great pains in initiating
and sustaining their relationships. In inculcating and
maintaining their friendships they fully comprehended
the vital import of diligence.*

"There is no man so imperfect that we cannot have for him a very perfect friendship, when we are loved by him, and when we have a truly noble and generous soul."

Rene Descartes, 1596-1650

"Short visits make long friends."

Hilaire Belloc, 1870-1953

"The more arguments you win the fewer friends you will have."

Abraham Lincoln, 1809-1865

"There run and caper and collide only four characters, who seem to sum up the four ultimate types of our existence—from which we must find our friends and enemies in this life. These four figures are: St. George, the dragon, the Princess offered to the dragon, and the father of the princess who did the offering. You have everything in those figures: active virtue destroying evil; passive virtue enduring evil; ignorance or convention permitting evil; and evil. In these four figures also can be found the real and sane limits of toleration. I admire St. George for being so sincere in his wish to save the Princess's life; I am ready to admire the Princess's wish to be eaten by the dragon as part of her religious and civic duties, if a bit perverse; I am even ready to admire the sincerity of the silly old potentate who gave up his daughter to a dragon because it had always been done in his set. But there is a limit; and I refuse to admire the dragon because he regarded the Princess with a sincere enthusiasm."

G.K. Chesterton, 1874-1936

"Don't worry about knowing people, just make your-self worth knowing."

Theodore Roosevelt, 1858-1919

"A person who has a many of friends either has a lot of money or is a good listener."

H.L. Mencken, 1880-1956

"Friendship of a kind that cannot easily be reversed tomorrow must have its roots in common interests and shared beliefs, and in some personal feeling."

John Laidlaw 1832-1906

"Men trust an ordinary man because they trust themselves. But men trust a great man because they do not
trust themselves. And hence the worship of great men
always appears in times of weakness and cowardice;
we never hear of great men until the time when all
other men are small."

G.K. Chesterton, 1874-1936

"Reprove not, in their wrath, excited men; good
counsel comes all out of season then: but when their
fury is appeased and past, they will perceive their
faults, and mend at last."

John Randolph, 1773-1833

Full many a glorious morning have I seen
Flatter the mountain tops with sovereign eye,
Kissing with golden face the meadows green,
Gilding pale streams with heavenly alchemy;
Anon permit the basest clouds to ride
With ugly rack on his celestial face,
And from the forlorn world his visage hide,
Stealing unseen to west with this disgrace.
Even so my sun one early morn did shine
With all triumphant splendor on my brow;
But out, alack, he was but one hour mine;
The region cloud hath masked him from me now.
  Yet him for this my love no whit disdaineth:
  Suns of the world may stain when heaven's sun
staineth.

William Shakespeare, c.1564-1616

Have you had a kindness shown?
    Pass it on;
'Twas not given for thee alone.

Let it travel down the years,
    Pass it on;
Let it wipe another's tears.

Offer to hearts a lilting dance,
    Pass it on;
With but a smile and glance.

Grace in friendship nears,
    Pass it on;
Till in Heaven the deed appears.

    Pass it on; indeed,
    Pass it on.
                    ❦ *John Duns, 1820-1909* ❧

"A bad conscience has a good memory."
H.G. Wells, 1866-1947

"Speak when you are angry and it will be the very finest speech you will ever regret. The greatest remedy for anger is delay. Indeed, a display of temper is the weak man's imitation of strength."
Raymond Asquith, 1875-1916

"I find friendship to be like wine, raw when new, ripened with age, the true old man's milk and restorative cordial."
Thomas Jefferson, 1743-1826

"An angry man is seldom reasonable; a reasonable man is seldom angry. Wrath has no place in friendship else friendship cease altogether."

Sir Walter Scott, 1771-1832

"There is a friend that sticketh closer than a brother."

King Solomon, c. 1000 BC

ALEXANDER STEPHENS, 1812-1883
AND ABRAHAM LINCOLN, 1809-1865

Opposed to secession prior to the hostilities and a strong proponent
for peace all throughout them, Alexander Stephens was an unlikely
prospect for the vice-presidency of the Confederacy during the tempestuous War Between the States. The Georgia congressman had
strong personal and political ties to the old Whig party in the North
and thus was intimate with many of the men he was later forced by
regrettable circumstances to oppose. Like so many of the leading
Southerners—Robert E. Lee, Stonewall Jackson, and Jefferson Davis
among them—he cherished his connections to the federal union of
states and to the gentlemen he had served with for so many years in
Washington.

Thus when his duty bade him home to join his fellow countrymen in what turned out to be a futile quest for independence, he left
Capitol Hill burdened with great sadness and foreboding. He
offered his farewell to friends and foes alike with sober graciousness.
Although his departure was not as dramatic as that of Jefferson
Davis, men from both North and South recalled that Stephens stood
out as a consummate gentleman.

He would later write: "It was my bounden duty to maintain honorable opposition to the ill forces of disintegration yet with all the dignity of Christian profession intact. To prosecute the path of liberty in an unwholesome or unwinsome manner is a despicable slight upon the name of freedom."

As the fledgling Confederate nation's Vice-President, he found himself at the head of a vaguely defined anti-administration party. Now at odds not only with his friends in the North but with many of his comrades in the South as well, Stephens again conducted himself with grace and civility. Though he was stalwart in defense of his convictions, he remained honorably chivalrous in all his personal dealings.

Interestingly, it was this chivalrous character that first endeared him to one of his oldest and dearest friends: Abraham Lincoln. Stephens grasped a principle that often seems to get lost amidst the passion of cultural or political tumult: the right thing done in the wrong way is no less pernicious than the wrong thing. And therein lay his remarkable capacity to maintain friendships over ideological lines—and even battle lines.

The contrasts between Stephens and Lincoln were obvious

enough. Stephens was a Southern defender of State sovereignty while Lincoln was a Northern advocate of Federal hegemony. Stephens was a conservative from the old democratic and republican school; Lincoln was a liberal from the new progressive and nationalist school. Stephens was an urbane scholar of some renown; Lincoln was a self-educated backwoods lawyer. Stephens was devout throughout his life, and for a time even studied for the Presbyterian ministry; Lincoln was a belligerent skeptic and only came to have Christian convictions following the tragedy of Gettysburg. Stephens had been successful all of his life in business, marriage, family, community, and politics; Lincoln suffered a long string of failures, sorrows, and humiliations in business, marriage, family, community, and politics. Lincoln's lanky and rugged frame stood out in any crowd; Stephens was extraordinarily diminutive and frail.

A villain to some, a hero to others, Lincoln undoubtedly attained greatness—but only in retrospect. In all history there is no more dramatic example of the times making a man rather than a man making the times than his legendary rise from obscurity to the Presidency of the shattered Union. Every conceivable obstacle was there before him: humble birth, ignorance, poverty, and life in the wilderness of the frontier; he was completely without advantages or connections; he was too human ever to be a favorite of the professional politicians; he was too enigmatic, too philosophical, too humorous ever to be a great popular figure.

He was born in rough and humble circumstances—in rural Kentucky. His mother died when he was eight and his father, a migratory farm worker and craftsman was in and out of trouble all his life. Thus Lincoln, bore the weight of poverty and shame. He tried a number of ventures before he found success in law and politics—all of them distinct and profound failures. In fact, according to biographer Carl Sandburg, his life was composed of "one calamity after another." Historian Webb Garrison describes the many paradoxes of the man: his unremitting separatism if not racism toward blacks, his reticence to end slavery even after the political ploy of the Emancipation Proclamation—which of course effected no emancipation whatsoever—his abrogation of innumerable constitutional standards and guarantees, and his absolute refusal to a negotiated peace settlement. But the most beguiling enigma of this complex man of genius, according to Garrison, was his uncompromising commitment to enforced union at all costs.

Stephens and Lincoln first met when they served together in the House of Representatives—Stephens served from 1843-1860 while Lincoln served only one term from 1847-1849. The two men seemed to be polar opposites in background, taste, interest, and political opinion. Yet they immediately found an appreciation for one another's company. Stephens enjoyed his friend's sense of humor and self-depreciating demeanor—a rarity in Washington. Lincoln appreciated his friend's remarkable grasp of history, literature, civics, and law. Though they made for an odd sight, they were an encouragement and a comfort to one another.

Lincoln's tacit support for the socialist revolutions wracking Europe at the time ultimately cost him his seat in Congress—he was advised by the party establishment not to run for re-election. It did not cost him his friendship with Stephens, however. The two men maintained a lively correspondence for as long as both of them were alive.

The regard Stephens had for his friend did not alter his political convictions, however. Indeed, Stephens was a strong supporter of Stephen A. Douglas—the great cross-state rival of Lincoln. But neither did that fact cause the friends to drift apart. In some ways their adversarial politics may have actually strengthened their personal relationship—much to the dismay of their other friends and acquaintances.

Somehow Lincoln was nominated for the Presidency—as the second choice of many; and with less than a majority of the popular vote he managed to be elected in 1860. Out of those early years of poverty and trial emerged a man uniquely prepared to wage a devastating war against many of his former friends and colleagues—a man of haunting transparency, a man with a probing conscience and a penetrating intellect, a man of deep humanity. After the first ineffectual and indecisive eighteen months in office Lincoln became a strong, effective leader—firm, unrelenting, and brutal in the prosecution of both war and politics. But, above all, he proved to be a man of vision. He saw the United States in its largest dimension—as a noble experiment in self-determination which had to be preserved even if that meant violating the principles of self-determination. In the long history of tyranny and oppression, he believed that the American democracy was man's great hope and that it must be saved even if resort had to be made to non-democratic coercion. To him the great ideal of democracy overshadowed the practical realities of democracy.

Lincoln's profound conviction of the enduring value of this experiment in a unified government sustained him throughout the long years of war. On the battlefield at Gettysburg it moved him to give the world a glimpse of his vision of the country's true greatness: "a nation conceived in liberty and dedicated to the proposition that all men are created equal." And it moved him to enunciate his ultimate reason for striving to preserve the Union: that "government of the people, by the people, and for the people shall not perish from the earth." One of the truly great political and human statements of all time, the Gettysburg Address reveals the both the ironic complexity and the coarse nobility that mark Lincoln as a legendary figure in American life and culture.

Meanwhile, Stephens—who had never supported secession—was stirred by the changes he was beginning to see in his dejected and discouraged friend to pursue a path of peace. From the end of 1863 to the beginning of 1865 he communicated with Lincoln several times in an attempt to get serious peace talks underway. His hope was either to secure Confederate independence or, better yet, to restore affairs to the status quo of 1860. In February of 1865 he headed a Southern peace commission and met with Lincoln. Both men were encouraged by the initial talks.

But of course, all hopes of a negotiated peace were dashed in April when first, Lee surrendered at Appomattox, and then five days later, Lincoln was assassinated at Ford's Theater in Washington.

In later years Stephens served his state as a congressman, governor, publisher, professor, and civil rights advocate. He forever rued the tragic loss of his friend—both for his own sake and for that of the nation. Indeed, he believed that the bonds of friendship they had shared might well have served to bring healing between the sundered regions and the divided land. At the very least, he was convinced that the crushing, cruel hand of Reconstruction could have been avoided if only Lincoln had lived and their friendship had continued—as most assuredly it would have.

He was convinced that the destiny of the nation actually hung in the balance of a friendship.

Discernment

*F*riendships don't just happen. They must be nurtured over time. They require a substantial investment of time, energy, and affection. As a result, they ultimately alter who we are and what we do. All the more reason to choose our friends carefully. Throughout history wise men and women have cautioned that without the exercise of discernment our relationships can actually wreak havoc in our lives.

"People are judged by both the company they keep and the company they keep away from."
◦{ Bonnie Prince Charlie, 1720-1788 }◦

"Our greatest wealth is not measured in terms of riches but relationships. Likewise, our greatest debts are incurred because of wastrel companions."
◦{ Oliver Cromwell, 1599-1658 }◦

"You can choose your friends, but you can have only one mother."

⊕ Hilaire Belloc, 1870-1953 ⊕

"Where you are liberal of your loves and counsels, be sure you be not loose; for those you make friends and give your heart to, when they once perceive the least rub in your fortunes, fall away like water from ye, never found again but where they mean to sink ye."

⊕ William Shakespeare, c.1564-1616 ⊕

"Bad company corrupts good character."
Paul of Tarsus, c. 10-65

"Books and friends should be few but good."
Patrick Henry, 1736-1799

"One friend in a lifetime is much; two are many;
three are hardly possible."
Henry Adams, 1838-1918

"Be slow in choosing a friend, slower in changing."
Benjamin Franklin, 1706-1790

"Fate chooses your relations, you choose your friends."
Christopher Wren, 1632-1723

"Be courteous to all, but intimate with few, and let those few be well tried before you give them your confidence. True friendship is a plant of slow growth, and must undergo and withstand the shocks of adversity before it is entitled to the appellation."
George Washington, 1732-1799

"I prefer to strive in bravery with the bravest, rather than in wealth with the wealthiest, or in greed with the greediest."

Plutarch, c.46-120

"Associate yourself with men of good quality if you esteem your own reputation; for tis better to be alone than in bad company."

George Washington, 1732-1799

"If a man does not make new acquaintances as he advances through life, he will soon find himself left alone."

Samuel Johnson, 1709-1784

"Two may walk together under the same roof for many years, yet never really meet; and two others at first speech are old friends."

Robert Howie, 1568-1646

"Poets and friends are born to what they are."

Alexander Stephens, 1812-1883

"A man with a definite belief always appears bizarre, because he does not change with the world; he has climbed into a fixed star and the earth whizzes below him like a zoetrope. Millions of mild black-coated men call themselves sane and sensible merely because they always catch the fashionable insanity, because they are hurried into madness after madness by the maelstrom of the world. The man with a definite belief is sure to be the truer friend."

G.K. Chesterton, 1874-1936

"With regard to the choice of friends, there is little to say; for a friend is never entirely and consciously chosen. A secret sympathy, the attraction of a thousand nameless qualities, a charm in the expression of countenance, even in the voice or manner, a similarity in circumstances—these are the things that begin attachment. Such things must be governed by discernment—the most difficult of all the tasks of self-control."

❧ *William Mitchell Ramsay, 1851-1939* ☙

You have, to be sure, known pain and fear,
And the anguish of failure and frustration are near;
Yet your eyes read companionship not distance,
Your home beckons forth, with no hint of resistance;
Indeed, your cloak, though threadbare, is half mine,
You are my friend, and I, most assuredly, am thine.

Tristan Gylberd, 1954-

"We must all measure ourselves by our friendships—
apart from the Scriptures, there is no surer measure
to be had in this poor fallen world."

Francis A. Schaeffer, 1912-1984

Beware of those with whom you rake and round,
Alert to dangers and snares,
And you will find that security and surety abound.
Listless discernment cares,
But little, so spent are lives upon the merest sound.
Thus the wise soul prepares,
And establishes an apprehension of solid ground.

Stephen Stewart, 1816-1888

TEDDY ROOSEVELT, 1858-1919
AND HENRY CABOT LODGE, 1850-1924

According to Shakespeare, "Talkers are no good doers." But there can be little doubt that Theodore Roosevelt violated that rule. Certainly he was a talker. He was an avid conversationalist, speechmaker, and communicator—perhaps among the most prolific men of this century. But he was hardly full of hot air. Though a talker, he was also a remarkable good doer.

Before his fiftieth birthday he had served as a New York State Legislator, the Under-Secretary of the Navy, Police Commissioner for the City of New York, US. Civil Service Commissioner, the Governor of the State of New York, the Vice-President under William McKinley, a Colonel in the US. Army, and two terms as the President of the United States. In addition, he had run a cattle ranch in the Dakota Territories, served as a reporter and editor for several journals, newspapers, and magazines, and conducted scientific expeditions on four continents.

As if all that were not enough, he read at least five books every week of his life—and wrote nearly sixty on a dizzying array of subjects. He enjoyed hunting, boxing, and wrestling. He was an amateur taxidermist, botanist, ornithologist, and astronomer. He was a devoted family man who lovingly raised five children. He enjoyed a life-long romance with his wife. And as a committed Christian he often taught a Sunday School class in his Dutch Reformed Church.

Amazingly, he never considered himself a particularly driven man. Instead, he believed that he was simply fulfilling his various duties—to God, to country, and to family. He had a strong sense of calling that motivated him to levels of high achievement in every area of his life. As he said: "The strenuous life is the fruit of a peculiar view of providence—one that calls us to a kind of holy guardianship, of high priesthood, and of societal responsibility. That is the secret of America's great vitality. That is the heart of my own endeavors in this world."

It is not surprising then to discover that Roosevelt was a man of enormous social skills. He had a compelling personal charisma that naturally drew others to himself. He was affable, gregarious, charming, and gracious. John Cater Rose once remarked that, "He gave every man he had talked with for five minutes the impression that he liked him very much."

He was a fascinating conversationalist. He was so remarkably well-informed that he could speak intelligently about almost any subject at length. But he by no means dominated discussions. Indeed he was an avid listener who often remained rather quiet in large public settings. He had a knack for bringing out the best in others. Thus, according to Albert Schauffler: "Though a brilliant, humorous, high-powered talker, he was more ear than mouth. On the slightest indication that another had anything to contribute, he would jam on all his verbal brakes. He was perhaps the most creative listener I have ever encountered. If we all had such audiences, we would continually excel ourselves."

He was a great encourager. He liked nothing better than to see others succeed. He marveled, even reveled, in the manifest gifts of others. And he was abundantly profusive in his praise of their achievements. As Irvin Cobb put it, "You had to hate Roosevelt a whole lot to keep from loving him."

As a result, he was a great friend—and he attracted a great variety of intimates. From his schooldays at Harvard he maintained lifelong friendships with such men of culture and refinement as William Roscoe Thayer, Harry Shaw, and Minot Weld. From his years in the

West he maintained long-term relationships with rough and tumble cowboys like Bill Sewall, Will Dow, and Bill Merrifield. From the world of politics he gained the devotion of cunning strategists like Elihu Root, John Hay, and Howard Taft. He was close to a number of scientists like John Muir, C. Hart Merriam, and William Beebe, military men like Fitzhugh Lee, Leonard Wood, George Dewey, and writers like Jacob Riis, Rudyard Kipling, and Owen Wister. And all of them treasured his company and companionship as among the most significant in their lives.

He was loyal, compassionate, tender-hearted, and most of all, fun. He always remembered names, special occasions, and intimate details about conversations that made his friends feel a sense of supreme importance.

Amazingly though, Roosevelt was not a particularly social person. Though he dearly loved his friends, he always preferred a quiet night at home with Edith and the children to anything or anyone else. He did not enjoy going out. He was not a "joiner." And he was convinced that he was a poor "mixer." He hated big parties and important social occasions—especially if he knew that he was to be the center of attention, which he almost always was. "Huge banquets and such" were "horrid functions" in his eyes. He always felt that he would be "caught" by some dominating boor or "button-holed" by some dim acquaintance—and often begged Edith to keep an eye out to "rescue him" if necessary. For the more frivolous activities of organized society he felt only contempt. "My own family, good book, a roaring fire, and a simple meal on the porch, now that is my idea of a bully social event." Both he and Edith loathed staying in other people's homes. When he was traveling he much preferred what he called "an old fogey hotel." And his favorite restaurants were "often rather disreputable hole in the wall joints."

He was, in reality, an intensely private person. He had only a handful of genuinely close friends with whom he shared his most intimate concerns. Like anyone who is constantly thrust into the public eye, he was able to maintain a wide circle of relationships through a generous application of the social graces. But he simultaneously guarded his private affairs, maintaining genuine intimacy only with those whom he could trust implicitly.

Aside from his wife and children, Henry Cabot Lodge was his nearest and dearest friend.

Lodge was a wealthy Boston Brahmin—the scion of two of the

most distinguished families in New England. After short stints teaching at Harvard, practicing law, and holding local political office, he served in the United States Senate for more than thirty years. He was an expert in foreign affairs and served as the Chairman of the Senate's powerful International Relations Committee—where he gained fame following the First World War as a fierce opponent of any and all entangling alliances that might compromise the sovereignty of the United States. Indeed, Lodge almost single handedly caused the demise of Woodrow Wilson's pet project, the League of Nations. In addition though, he was an accomplished scholar and wrote or edited a number of important works, including a rich twelve-volume anthology of the world's greatest literary classics and definitive works on the pioneering thought of the great American Federalists Alexander Hamilton and Fisher Ames.

Lodge met Roosevelt when the young New York reformer first came to Washington as a Civil Service Commissioner in 1889. They became fast friends. Both were irrepressible polymaths—interested in a thousand different subjects, disciplines, and issues. Both had avid interests in history—Roosevelt had just completed his biographies of Thomas Hart Benton and Gouverneur Morris and Lodge had just completed his biographies of George Washington and Daniel Webster for the same publisher. They shared a common philosophical and political outlook. And both were deeply devout and scrupulously moral—then as now, rather rare traits in Washington.

They spent as much time together as their busy careers would allow. They would often walk together through Rock Creek Park. They enjoyed gathering their families together for dinner. They joined one another for vacations either at Roosevelt's home on Long Island or Lodge's on Cape Cod. According to Edith, the two men were "like brothers." She said they "talked a blue streak" and often "lost themselves in the deep canyons of their wild intellectual pursuits." Roosevelt's son Kermit, who accompanied his father on two dangerous year-long expeditions to the heart of Africa and along the unexplored Amazon commented that Lodge knew his father "better than anyone alive, save Mother. At some deep level, they were soul mates. Father would have assuredly accomplished much in his life, but perhaps the Senator magnified and multiplied those accomplishments through his camaraderie, accountability, and encouragement."

In later years, the two men would collaborate on innumerable campaigns, legislative programs, and international initiatives, but in 1895 they co-wrote a collection of historical profiles and vignettes, Hero Tales of American History. It was their favorite project—and remained so throughout their lives. Reading it today reveals much about the strength that both men drew from their relationship. Ted, the first-born of Roosevelt's brood asserts, "That book not only provides portraits of a fistful of American heroes, it portrays the way a collaborative friendship can shape the destiny of a nation."

When the great old lion of American politics died on January 1919, all of America was stricken with grief. The funeral of Theodore Roosevelt was a quiet, private affair at Oyster Bay within sight of his beloved Sagamore Hill home. It was there, accompanied by the hushed strains of his favorite hymn—George Keith's *How Firm a Foundation*—that he was laid to rest. But America—indeed the world—would not be content with such a private end to such a public life. Hundreds, perhaps even thousands, of memorial services were held all across the land. Messages of grief, sorrow, and condolence poured in from around the globe—from kings and princes to paupers and pedestrians. Accolades, eulogies, tributes, and reminiscences were published, broadcast, and announced at every turn. It seemed everyone, from the mighty to the obscure, desired to have their say about the great man. But it seemed everyone also wanted to hear from Henry Cabot Lodge, a friend who had known this great *Nephiliam* like no other.

On February 9, 1919, a memorial service was held in Congress—and afterwards a reverent prayer vigil was held. Lodge spoke in halting tones of his remarkable beloved friend: "He had a touch of the knight errant in his daily life, although he would have never admitted it; but it was there. It was not visible in the medieval form of shining armor and dazzling tournaments but in the never-ceasing effort to help the poor and oppressed, to defend and protect women and children, to right the wronged and succor the downtrodden. Passing by on the other side was not a mode of travel through life ever possible to him; and yet he was as far distant from the professional philanthropist or the liberal do-gooder as could well be imagined, for all he tried to do to help his fellow men he regarded as a part of the day's work to be done and not talked about. No man ever prized sentiment or hated sentimentality more than he. He preached unceasingly the familiar morals which lie at the bottom of both family and public life. The blood of some ancestral Scotch Covenanter or of some Dutch Reformed preacher facing down tyranny was in his veins, and with his large opportunities and vast audiences he was always ready to appeal for justice and righteousness. But his own particular ideals he never attempted to thrust upon the world until the day came when they were to be translated into realities of personal action."

He concluded, saying: "Indeed, the absolute purity and integrity of his family life—where those ideals first met the test of authenticity—tell us why the pride and interest which his fellow countrymen felt in him were always touched with the warm light of love. In the home so dear to him, in his sleep, death came, and so, Valiant-for-Truth passed over and all the trumpets sounded for him on the other side."

· BEST FRIENDS ·

Duty

*F*riends are honest with each another. They hold each other
accountable. They stand together through thick and thin. They
care for each another despite all the years and all the miles—
years and miles that might cause mere acquaintances to drift
apart and lose touch. Friends are not wowed by the razzle-
dazzle or deterred by the dreary-dismal. They take their
relationship seriously. In short, friendship is a responsibility.
It is a duty. It requires work, commitment, sacrifice, and
diligence—a fact that wise men and women through
the ages have always known.

"Friendship is a responsibility, not an opportunity."
Calvin Coolidge, 1872-1933

"A man cannot be said to succeed in this life who does not satisfy one friend."
Henry David Thoreau, 1817-1862

"The doer of the favor is the firmer friend of the two, in order by continued kindness to keep the recipient in his debt; while the debtor feels less keenly from the very consciousness that the return he makes will be repayment, not a free gift."
Thucydides, c.460-400 BC

"A friend's only gift is himself. To praise the utility of friendship, as the ancients so often did, and to regard it as a political institution justified, like victory or government, by its material results, is to lose one's moral bearings. We are not to look now for what makes friendships useful, but for whatever may be found in friendship that may lend utility to life."

George Santayana, 1863-1952

"A man, sir, should keep his friendships in constant repair."

Samuel Johnson, 1709-1784

"We should not let the grass grow on the path of friendship."

St. Augustine, 354-430

"The only way to have a friend is to be one."

◦{ Ralph Waldo Emerson, 1803-1882 }◦

"What makes the Dead Sea dead? It is all the time receiving, but never giving out anything. Why is it that so many friendships grow cold? Perhaps it is because they too are all the time receiving, never giving."

◦{ Dwight L. Moody, 1837-1899 }◦

"There is nothing in all the world so precious as a friend who is at once wise and true."

◦{ John Buchan, 1875-1940 }◦

"A true friend unbosoms freely, advises justly, assists readily, adventures boldly, takes all patiently, defends courageously, and continues a friend unchangeably."

William Penn, 1644-1718

"We love those who know the worst of us and don't turn their faces away."

John Buchan, 1875-1940

"A friend in deed is a friend indeed."

Abraham Lincoln, 1809-1865

Stern daughter of the Voice of God!
O Duty! If that name thou love,
Who art a light to guide a rod
To check the erring and reprove;

Thou, who art victory and law
When empty terrors overawe;
From vain temptations dost set free;
And calm'st the weary strife of frail humanity!

These are who ask not if thine eye
Be on them; who, in love and truth,
Where no misgiving is, rely
Upon the genial sense of youth:

Glad hearts! Without reproach or blot;
Who do thy work, and know it not:
O, if through confidence misplaced
They fail, thy saving arms around them cast.

Serene will be our days and bright,
And happy will our nature be,
When love is an unerring light,
And joy its own security.

And they a blissful course may hold
Even now, who, not unwisely bold,
Live in the spirit of this creed;
Yet seek thy support, according to need.

William Wordsworth, 1770-1850

"Better be a nettle in the side of your friend than his echo."

ᴇᴊ *Ralph Waldo Emerson, 1803-1882* ⅟ₑ

"There can be no friendship where there is no freedom. Friendship loves a free air, and will not be fenced up in straight and narrow enclosures."

ᴇᴊ *William Penn, 1644-1718* ⅟ₑ

"The more we love our friends the less we flatter them; it is by excusing nothing that pure love shows itself."

ᴇᴊ *H.L. Mencken, 1880-1956* ⅟ₑ

"Greater love hath no man than this, that he lay down his life for his friends."

Jesus, John 15:13

"Ultimately a man is not judged by what he has done or what he has written but who he has influenced—and who has influenced him."

Andrew Nelson Lytle, 1902-1996

"A genuine friend is always willing to help us, even when it hurts us."

Brother Bryan, 1863-1941

"Write down the advice of him who loves you, though you like it not at present."

Ben Johnson, 1573-1637

JOHN BUNYAN, 1628-1688
AND ELIZABETH BUNYAN, 1639-1694

The great Victorian preacher, Charles Spurgeon, read it more than a hundred times. E.M. Bounds kept a copy by his bedside and read from it every night before retiring. Stonewall Jackson kept a copy in his knapsack throughout his Southern campaigns. D.L. Moody and Ira Sankey shared favorite passages from it each night before beginning their evangelistic services. In the seventeenth century, John Owen said it was "a masterpiece of Christian devotion." In the eighteenth century, Patrick Henry called it "a veritable Christian classic." In the nineteenth century, Lord Shaftesbury asserted that it was "indispensable in the arsenal of spiritual warfare." In our own century its enduring value was affirmed by C.S. Lewis who said it was "a literary and spiritual masterpiece." Translated into more languages than any other book save the Bible, it is utterly unique among the literary creations of men. It is *Pilgrim's Progress*, a fanciful allegory of the Christian life written primarily from a prison cell midway through the seventeenth century by John Bunyan.

The son of a poor brazier, born in 1628, Bunyan was a witness to some of the momentous events in English history: the civil war, the regicide of King Charles, the Cromwell protectorate, the great fire, the restoration of the monarchy, and the great Puritan purge. Those were tumultuous days—days that left an indelible mark of change upon the souls of both men and nations. Bunyan was no exception. After a dramatic adult conversion, he immersed himself in the life and work of a very small non-conformist congregation.

After the demise of the protectorate and the subsequent restoration of the monarchy in 1660, persecutions were launched against all but established state churches. It was widely understood that religion was the primary influence on the nature and structure of culture. Preaching was considered to be a powerful force that had both eternal and temporal dimensions. Thus, they rightly predicted that a faithful exposition of the Bible would have immediate political as well as spiritual ramifications. Conservative Anglicans and Puritans thought that allowing unauthorized or unlearned men to preach would undermine the whole social fabric. They comprehended only too well the dynamic significance of worldviews.

For nearly a decade, Bunyan had served as an unordained itinerant preacher and had frequently taken part in highly visible theological controversies. It was natural that the new governmental restrictions would focus on him. Thus, he was arrested for preaching to "unlawful assemblies and conventicles."

The judges who were assigned to his case were all ex-royalists, most of whom had suffered fines, sequestrations, and even imprisonments during the Interregnum. They threatened and cajoled Bunyan, but he was unshakable. Finally, in frustration, they told him they would not release him from custody until he was willing to foreswear his illegal preaching. And so, he was sent to the county gaol where he spent twelve long years—recalcitrant to the end.

Bunyan had been married at the time of this first arrest—there would be many more—less than six months. His wife, Elizabeth, was pregnant at the time. Now she was solely responsible for the maintenance of their household and the care of four children from Bunyan's previous marriage. In addition, she had to care for her husband in the gaol—in those days families were responsible for all meals, clothing, and sustenance. By all counts she proved to be a remarkably longsuffering helpmeet for him—despite the fact that in their first twenty years of marriage Bunyan was able to be at home less than three.

Though little is known about her background prior to her marriage, much may be inferred from Bunyan's occasional letters and diary entries. She was apparently from a humble but pious background, not at all unlike her husband. Tempered by suffering and privation, bolstered by persecution and stigmatization, and motivated by faith and devotion, she was a voice of encouragement, comfort, and inspiration to her husband. Their marriage was marked by the strong bonds of covenantal friendship as well as the emotional bonds of love.

Because of her strong exhortations to use his time of incarceration wisely, he began writing the allegorical *Pilgrim's Progress* as a sort of spiritual autobiography. It describes his temptations, trials, frustrations as well as his determination to risk all for the sake of spiritual integrity and the quest for righteousness.

Like *The Canterbury Tales, Don Quixote, The Aneid,* and even *The Inferno,* the story is written as a travelogue—the hero embarks on a great adventure and must face many perils along the way until at long last he arrives at his destination or meets his destiny. In this case, brave Christian leaves his secure home in search of the Celestial City. Along the way he meets a vast array of characters,

both good and evil, in an alternating landscape of dizzying depriva-
tion and dazzling debauchery.

Around the rough framework of Christian's salvation and early
discipleship is an episodic series of fearsome and fast-paced battles,
discoveries, and encounters. He guides us through Puritan England's
fairs, fields, and foibles. And he uncovers its competing psychologies,
passions, and perplexities. But perhaps the liveliest and the most
stimulating scenes in the story are the characterizations of hypocrites
and villains that Christian meets along the way. His loving, insightful, and exact observations of human nature are fiercely disarming
and satirically precise. Bunyan's great universal appeal is this unerring genius in capturing the essence of everyday eccentricities.

Next to the Bible, it became the best-loved and most-read book
during the first three hundred years of American colonial and
national life. Its plot was familiar to every school child. Its characters
became cultural icons. Its imagery was seamlessly woven into the art,
music, literature, and ideas of the people.

The opening lines of the saga were etched into the memories of
untold thousands and became a kind of yard-stick against which to
measure literary and devotional excellence: "As I walked through the

wilderness of this world, I lighted on a certain place where was a
den, and I laid me down in that place to sleep, and as I slept I
dreamed a dream. I dreamed, and behold I saw a man clothed in
rags, standing in a certain place, with his face from his own house, a
book in his hand, and a great burden on his back. I looked and saw
him open the book, and read therein; and as he read he wept and
trembled, and not being able to longer to contain, he brake out with
a lamentable cry, saying: What shall I do?"

The first section of the book was published in 1678. It essentially
detailed the trials and tribulations of a young man who left behind
his beloved wife and home as he made his way through the treacher-
ous world. He was a spiritual pilgrim—journeying toward his ultimate home, the Celestial City. Along the way he passed through
such tempestuous places as Vanity Fair, the Slough of Despond,
Strait Gate, the Hill of Difficulty, Delectable Mountains, By-Path
Meadow, Lucre Hill, Doubting Castle, and Mount Caution. Those
inhospitable locales were populated by a variety of carefully drawn
villains such as Obstinate, Pliable, Mr. Worldly-Wiseman, Mistrust,
Timorous, Wanton, Talkative, Envy, Mr. Money-Love, Faint-Heart,
and Little-Faith. Despite the fact that he was helped from time to

time by a whole host of heroic characters such as Evangelist, Faithful, Good Will, Hopeful, Knowledge, Experience, Watchful, and Sincere, the hapless pilgrim had to struggle through one difficulty or distraction after another. Again and again he was forced to decide between compromise or faithfulness, between accommodation with the world or holy perseverance, between the wide way to destruction or the narrow road to glory. After overcoming a number of chilling risks and hazards, the story was ultimately resolved—like virtually all great classic works of literature—with a happy ending.

Interestingly, the second part of the great work was published in 1684. It described the journey of the pilgrim's wife as she followed in her husband's footsteps. Lead by the warrior Greatheart, an archetype of the ideal Puritan pastor, she sees all the remarkable battlefields where her beloved husband vanquished giants and demons. She has her own adventures along the way, but unlike the lonely journey Christian was forced to take, Christiana is able to follow a path that has already been forged for her. Essentially the story is a tender examination of John and Elizabeth Bunyan's own struggles—in their family, in their faith, and in their community. And the picture that emerges is one of deep and abiding love, understanding, loyalty, commitment, and, of course, friendship.

The two parts of the book were published together shortly afterward and became an immediate sensation. Though written in a coarse, speech-pattered prose—a far cry from the polite literary convention of the seventeenth century—the book was almost immediately acclaimed as a masterpiece of imagination and inspiration. Even those Christians who chafed a bit at Bunyan's gallant Puritan theology, his stalwart Calvinistic doctrine, and his intrepid Non-Conformist practice readily identified with his beautifully realized vision of life in this poor fallen world. What appeared on the surface to be little more than an episodic series of adventures or a blithe narrative of folk-tale ups and downs, was in fact, a penetrating portrayal of the universal human experience—of faith in the face of suppression, of love in the face of temptation, and of friendship in the face of separation.

Pilgrim's Progress struck a nerve. Drawing from obvious autobiographical details, Bunyan threw the searchlight of understanding on the soul of Everyman. As literary critic Roger Sharrock said: "A seventeenth-century Calvinist sat down to write a tract and produced a folk-epic of the universal religious imagination instead."

In the center of Bedford, England there stands a statue of Bunyan carrying a tinker's burden upon his back and a Bible in his hand. It marks the place where that great Puritan spent the long years of his imprisonment for the offense of teaching and preaching without proper state certification. Near the foot of the statue is a little bronze plaque. On it are engraved the words of the prosecutor—the Lord Judge Magistrate of Bedford—spoken at Bunyan's sentencing in 1673. The judge said: "At last we are done with this tinker and his cause. Never more will he plague us: for his name, locked away as surely as he, shall be forgotten, as surely as he. Done we are, and all eternity with him."

Of course, it is not Bunyan that is forgotten. Instead, it is the Lord Judge Magistrate of Bedford that remains unnamed and unremembered.

There is no monument to Elizabeth there. There is no mention of her courage, her tenacity, or her forbearance through the long years that enabled her husband's message to ring out across the vast chasm of time and distance. But for any who know of her story of friendship, love, and grace, her presence is surely felt. And thus, she is by no means forgotten either.

Forbearance

There are no perfect friendships because, alas, there are no perfect people. All of us have irritating habits, idiosyncrasies, wonts, dispositions, proclivities, manners, demeanors, and quirks. Our friends must of necessity bear with us in charity and patience. They must have generous forbearance. Likewise, we must reciprocate. Through the ages, the best friendships have not been those where men and women have been especially well suited, one toward another, but where they have been especially well accredited, one toward another.

"Treat your friends like family and your family like friends."

Cotton Mather, 1663-1728

"You never know the best about men until you know the worst about them."

G.K. Chesterton, 1874-1936

"Friendship affords us its undivided attentions."

Jonathan Edwards, 1703-1758

I land ha'e thought, my youthfu' friend,
A something to have sent you,
Though it should serve nae other end
Than just a kind memento;
But how the subject theme may gang,
Let time and chance determine;
Perhaps it may turn out a sang,
Perhaps turn out a sermon.

Ye'll try the world soon, my lad
And, Andrew dear, believe me,
Ye'll find mankind an unco squad,
And muckle they might grieve ye:
For care and trouble set your thought,
E'en when your end's attained;
And a' your views may come to nought,
Where every nerve is strained.

I'll no say men are villains a'
The real, hardened wicked,
Wha ha'e nae check but human law,
Are to a few restricted:
But och, mankind are unco weak,
An' little to be trusted;
If self the wavering balance shake,
It's rarely right adjusted!

Yet they wha fa' in fortune's strife,
Their fate we should na censure,
For still th' important end of life
They equally may answer;
A man may ha'e an honest heart,
Though poortith hourly stare him;
A man may tak' a neebor's part,
Yet nae ha'e cash to spare him.

Aye free, aff han your story tell,
When wi' a bosom crony;
But still keep something to yoursel'
Ye scarcely tell to ony.
Conceal yoursel' as weel's ye can,
Fra critical dissection;
But keek through every other man,
Wi' sharpened, sly inspection.

The sacred lowe o' weel-placed love,
Luxuriantly indulge it;
But never tempt th' illicit rove,
Though naething should divulge it.
I wave the quantum o' the sin,
The hazard of concealing:
But och! It hardens a' within,
And petrified the feeling!

The fear o' hell's a hangman's whip
To haud the wretch in order;
But where ye feel your honour grip,
Let that aye be your border;
Its slightest touches, instant pause;
Debar a' side pretences;
And resolutely keep its laws,
Uncaring consequences.

The Great Creator to revere,
Must sure become the creature;
But still the preaching cant forbear,
And e'en the rigid feature:
Yet ne'er with wits profane to range,
Be complaisance extended;
An atheist's laugh's a poor exchange
For Deity offended!

Robert Burns, 1759-1796

"We must develop and maintain the capacity to forgive. He who is devoid of the power to forgive is devoid of the power to love. There is some good in the worst of us and some evil in the best of us. When we discover this, we are less prone to hate our enemies."

Martin Luther King, Jr., 1929-1968

"Friendship rather chooseth harm to itself than offer it."

Sir Walter Raleigh, 1552-1618

"Let us no more contend, nor blame each other, blamed enough elsewhere, but strive in offices of love, how we may lighten each other's burden, in our share of woe."

John Milton, 1608-1674

Longsuffering: we admire that quality a great deal more than we practice it. We admire longsuffering in the schoolmaster, in the regent mother, in the creditor to whom we owe a debt. It inspires almost the dignity of perfect beauty. A man who will let you abuse him, a man who will let you cheat him even, a man who forgets today what you said or did yesterday—his longsuffering, oh, how beautiful it is. It is a patience that is not easily provoked and thinketh no evil. Yet look at that matron who through the years of early life inherited bereavements and sorrows, the thinning out of the precious flock, the dishonored name of the husband, the death, the rolling upon her of the responsibility of rearing the whole flock, the unwearied fidelity, the inexhaustible patience, furrow after furrow that experience is ploughing upon her brow; at last the children had come to ripeness, and they in their turn are lifting her out of her trouble, and she sits serene at the end of life more beautiful than the going down of the sun. Is there any object in life more beautiful than the going down of the sun. Is there any object in life that a man may look upon that is more beautiful than longsuffering.

Henry Ward Beecher, 1813-1887

"There is no music in a rest, but there's the making of music in it. And people are always missing that part of the life melody, always talking of perseverance and courage and fortitude; but patience is the finest and worthiest part of fortitude, and the rarest too—even among friends."

John Ruskin, 1819-1900

"The love toward our fiends and neighbors must be like the pure and chaste love between bride and bridegroom, where faults are connived at and borne with, and only virtues are regarded."
Martin Luther, 1483-1546

JOHN BUCHAN, 1875-1940
AND THOMAS NELSON, 1874-1917

Like the plot in one of his best-selling novels, the life of John Buchan was full of improbable adventures and prodigious achievements. He was one of the most accomplished men of the twentieth century—he was by turns a successful barrister, a respected scholar, a popular journalist, a trusted diplomat, a prolific author, an efficient colonial administrator, an innovative publisher, a progressive politician, a relentless reformer, and an active churchman. Best known for his historical romances and thrilling spy novels—he practically invented the genre—he was also the author of more than a hundred non-fiction works, including an authoritative multi-volume history of the First World War and biographies of Oliver Cromwell, Caesar Augustus, Lord Montrose, and Walter Scott.

He was born in Scotland on August 26, 1875, the eldest son of a minister in the Presbyterian Free Church. He was of regal Scottish stock—a Countess of Buchan had crowned Robert the Bruce, an Earl of Buchan had avenged Joan of Arc as Constable of France, a Buchan of Auchmacoy had fallen at Flodden beside the King, and

another had led the Jacobite remnant after the death of Dundee—
but it was his early years in the strict Calvinistic manse that would
shape his worldview and stimulate his imagination for the rest of his
life. Following a brilliant academic career at the University of
Glasgow he transferred to Oxford.

It was there that he first met Tommie Nelson. The young Nelson
was an impressive fellow—Scot, scion of the great Edinburgh publishing enterprise founded by his grandfather. By all accounts he was
a man destined for great things. According to Buchan's autobiography, Nelson was a remarkable man and a remarkable friend: "It is
not easy to draw on a little canvas the man whose nature is large and
central and human, without cranks or oddities. The very simplicity
and wholesomeness of such souls defy an easy summary, for they are
as spacious in their effect as daylight or summer. Often we remember friends by a gesture, or a trick of expression, or by a favorite
phrase, or some nicety of manner. These were trivial things in our
friendship, but they spring first to the mind in the act of recollec-
tion. But with Tommie Nelson I do not find myself thinking of such
idiosyncrasies. I can recall many mannerisms of his, but it is only by
an effort of thought, for they do not run to meet the memory. His

presence warmed and lit up so big a region of life that in thinking of him one is overwhelmed by the multitude of things that he made better by simply existing among them. If you remove a fire from a hearth, you will remember the look, not so much of the blaze itself as of the whole room in its pleasant glow."

Nelson was the captain of the Oxford rugby team, president of the Scottish academic club, and like Buchan, a prolific reader and writer. He was an avid sportsman, again like Buchan, and a brilliant student. His piety, grace, and rugged good humor made him "the most popular man in the university."

Following their four years together at Oxford, the two men went their separate ways—Nelson back to Edinburgh to join the family business and Buchan to a varied career in journalism and civic affairs. Nevertheless, the two men often found opportunities to renew their intimate friendship—they vacationed together, wrote frequently, and whenever both were in London, whiled away many hours together in conversation and fellowship.

Always interested in politics, Buchan accepted an invitation to join the staff of Lord Milner, High Commissioner of South Africa following the Boer War. His efficient administrative reforms earned him a trusted place in His Majesty's court and his foreign dispatches earned him renown as one of the British Empire's finest correspondents.

Following his tenure in the foreign service he was offered lucrative posts at both the Nelson family firm and of the international news service Reuters. He naturally chose to go to work with his old friend. Later he would assert that those were the happiest years of his life. It was then that Buchan began his writing career in earnest, publishing several highly acclaimed novels and historical studies. When war broke out in Europe those halcyon days came to an end. Both men set aside their wide-ranging pursuits to enter the military—Buchan joined British Intelligence Corps as a department director; Nelson joined the tank corps. They were able to see each other several times during the course of the war, and each time afforded them immeasurable encouragement and refreshment. Alas, those happy times were cut off when on the last day of the fierce Battle of Arras Nelson was killed by a long-range shell across the German lines.

Scotland was grief-stricken. As his beloved friend would later recall: "His death made a bigger hole in the life of Scotland than that of any other man of his years. He was a rare being because he was so superbly normal, so wholly in tune with ordinary humanity, and therefore fitted to help in the difficult but not desperate life of man. In the case of others we might regret the premature loss of some peculiar talent; with Tommie we mourned especially the loss of a talent for living worthily and helping others to do likewise. It is the kind of great loss least easy to forget, and yet one which soon comes to be contemplated without pain, for he had succeeded most fully in life."

In the years that followed, Buchan would continue to be inspired—and even spurred on to greater accomplishment—by the memory of his dear friend who he described as "the Christian statesman extrordinaire."

After the First World War he was elected to Parliament representing the Scottish Universities, a position he held until 1935. Meanwhile he resumed his flourishing literary career—between 1922 and 1936 he averaged five books a year. For much of that time he was ranked among the world's best-selling authors alongside his friends and acquaintances Rudyard Kipling, Virginia Wolfe, G.K. Chesterton, Hilaire Belloc, and Hugh Walpole. Several of his books, including *The Thirty-Nine Steps, Prester John, Huntingtower,* and

John McNab were even made into full-length motion pictures by the likes of Alfred Hitchcock and Arthur Lammis. Though his work was popular, it often explored serious theological themes and profound human dilemmas. Indeed, according to T.E. Lawrence, he was "the greatest romancer of our blind and undeserving generation."

Throughout the busy activity of his career he maintained a vital interest in both his family and his faith. He was married in 1907 to Susan Grosvenor and together they had a daughter and three sons. Though always maintaining a busy schedule he made certain that his children remained a priority in their lives. Likewise, he was a faithful member of the Presbyterian Church, serving his congregation as a Bible study leader and elder for most of his adult life.

His political, cultural, and spiritual prominence made him an appropriate choice as the king's Lord High Commissioner to the General Assembly of the Church of Scotland for several years beginning in 1933. The post enabled him to promote the vital relationship between the dynamics of the Christian life and the preservation of Western Civilization—a relationship he believed was threatened by the hubris of modern secularism. It was a theme that resonated throughout all his work. "Our enemies are attacking more than our system of Christian morals on which our civilization is founded" he lamented. "They are attacking Christianity itself, and they are succeeding. Our great achievements in perfecting the scientific apparatus of life have tended to produce a mood of self-confidence and pride. We have too often become gross materialists in our outlook on life."

Despite this obvious twentieth century cultural retrogression, Buchan remained confident. "I believe that the challenge with which we are faced may restore us to that manly humility in the presence of the Unseen which alone gives power, " he said. "It may bring us back to God. In that case our victory is assured. The church of Christ is an anvil which has worn out many hammers. Our opponents may boast of their strength, but they do not realize what they have challenged."

His tireless activities on behalf of Christ and Crown brought him greater and greater prominence and despite deteriorating health he served as Curator of Oxford University Chest, Trustee of the National Library of Scotland, President of the Scottish Historical Society, and Chancellor of Edinburgh University.

In 1935 King George V ennobled him as the 1st Lord Tweedsmuir of Elsfield and—at the behest of Prime Minister Mackenzie King—was appointed the fifteenth Governor-General of Canada. Despite recurring ill-health Buchan threw himself into these new proconsular duties with especial fervor. Moving to Ottawa, he quickly fell in love with the great beauty and diversity of Canada—a land he called "God's manifestation of grace among the nations."

Always an avid outdoorsman, he toured every province and explored every aspect of Canadian life and culture. He lectured widely across the land, making strong pleas for vigilant national unity, keen historical awareness, and unflinching spiritual integrity. He constantly promoted Canadian arts and sciences—acting as an advocate for the nation's universities and establishing the Governor-General's Literary Awards. In the tumultuous days during the advent of the Second World War, he became a beloved symbol of faith, stability, and constancy in the face of great evil.

Thoughout all these crowded hours of life, his memory of his friend was never far from him. He would later lament that his drive to accomplish so much was "a poor attempt to compensate" a world which "had lost so great a talent in Tommie Nelson."

Buchan's sudden death on February 12, 1940 was caused by a freak injury following a fall in his official Ottawa residence, Rideau Hall. The sad news made front page headlines around the world from South Africa and Australia to Britain and the United States— but nowhere was he mourned as sincerely as in his adopted home. As the historian G.M. Trevelyan commented in the *Globe and Mail*, "I don't think I remember anyone who has died during my lifetime whose death ever had a more enviable outburst of sorrow and love and admiration, public and private. He was the Christian statesman extrordinaire."

It was an interesting choice of words—the very phrase that Buchan had used to describe his long lost friend. It was perhaps the most fitting tribute of all.

· BEST FRIENDS ·

Joy

*To have someone we can laugh with is a great gift.
A friend is thus a welcome companion in this poor fallen
world—a companion we can have fun with. Fellowship is an
essential element of a healthy, well-balanced, and productive
life. Happy then is the man who has known deep and
abiding friendship. For many of the great men and
women of the ages, the most obvious benefit of
friendship is the joy it offers.*

"It may be true that he travels farthest who travels alone; but the goal thus reached is not worth reaching."

Theodore Roosevelt, 1858-1919

"Friendship doubles our joy and halves our grief."

Dolly Madison, 1768-1849

"A merry heart does good, like medicine."

King Solomon, Proverbs 17:22

"Friendships, like geraniums, bloom in kitchens."
Peter Lorimer, 1812-1879

"When a friend speaks to me, whatever he says is interesting."
Jean Renoir, 1894-1979

"Friendship is the greatest enrichment that I have found."
Adlai Stevenson, 1900-1965

From quiet homes and first beginning,
   Out to the undiscovered ends,
There's nothing worth the wear of winning,
   But the laughter and love of friends.

Hilaire Belloc, 1870-1953

"The great man never loses his child's heart. What is true of the Kingdom of God must also be true in the affairs of men."

Kermit Roosevelt, 1889-1943

"The art of life is to know how to enjoy a little and to endure much."

William Hazlitt, 1778-1830

"Friendships ought to be founts of joy. Therein we find not only our truest companions but our truest selves. Therein we tap into the source for an authentic happiness, for it redounds to a providential provocation of all that is good and substantial and true. Let us not therefore take for granted or neglect for the sake of business this matter of friendship."

Jane Austen, 1775-1817

"Friendship is the vintage wine of a procreant fellowship. It is the sweet morsel of a kindred spirit. It is the aromatic salve of a sonorous intimacy. It is the delicate dessert of a fine providence. It is meat to the breast and balm to the soul. It is all that is good and just and right and true and needful. It is joy itself."

Soren Kierkegaard, 1813-1855

This day is called the feast of Crispian:
He that outlives this day, and comes safe home,
Will stand a tip-toe when this day is named,
And rouse him at the name of Crispian.
He that shall live this day and see old age,
Will yearly on the vigil feast his neighbors
And say 'Tomorrow is St. Crispian.'
Then he will strip his sleeve and show his scars,
And say, 'These wounds I had on Crispin's day.'
Old men forget; yet all shall be forgot,
But he'll remember with advantages
What feats he did that day. Then shall our names,
Familiar in his mouth as household words,
Harry the king, Bedford and Exeter,

Warwick and Talbot, Salisbury and Gloucester,
Be in their flowing cups freshly remembered.
This story shall the good man teach his son;
And Crispin Crispian shall ne'er go by,
From this day to the ending of the world,
But we in it shall be remembered;
We few, we happy few, we band of brothers;
For he today that sheds his blood with me
Shall be my brother; be he ne'er so vile
This day shall gentle his condition:
And gentlemen in England now abed
Shall think themselves accursed they were not here,
And hold their manhoods cheap whiles any speaks
That fought with us upon St. Crispin's day.

William Shakespeare, c. 1564-1616

I wonder if you really send
   Those dreams of you that come and go!
I like to say, "She thought of me,
   And I have known it." Is it so?

Though other friends walk by your side,
Yet sometimes it must surely be,
They wonder where your thoughts have gone
   Because I have you here with me.

And when the busy day is done
   And work is ended, voices cease
When everyone has said goodnight,
   In fading firelight, then in peace

I idly rest: you come to me,
   Your dear love holds me close to you.
If I could see you face to face
   It would not be more sweet and true
      ❧ *Sarah Orne Jewett, 1835-1882* ☙

"Reflect that life, like every other blessing, derives its value from its use alone. Similarly, friendship derives its merit from the intangibles of delectation."
      ❧ *Samuel Johnson, 1709-1784* ☙

AUGUSTINE, 354-430 AND MONICA, 327-383

One of the most remarkable men Africa ever produced—standing
shoulder to shoulder with such giants as Athanasius, Origen, and
Tertullian—was Augustine of Hippo. He would eventually prove to
be a pillar of Western thought—perhaps Christendom's single most
important cultural influence from the time of the Roman Empire
until the Reformation more than a thousand years later.

He was born in 354 at Tagaste—in present-day Algeria—of a
pagan father and a Christian mother. Monica, his mother, was a vital
and invigorating influence on him from his earliest remembrance.
She was unusually gifted—and determined to see her son advance.
She secured for him the best possible classical education—and then,
because he proved to be an able scholar, prodded him on toward
advanced studies. As a result, he studied rhetoric at the great
University of Carthage in order to become a lawyer, but later gave
up his plan to for a career in teaching. His study of rhetorical philosophy—with an emphasis on Platonism and Manichaenism—resulted
in a complete renunciation of Christianity. This very nearly broke
Monica's heart.

Even more grievous to her, Augustine began to live a self-con-fessedly debauched life—including keeping a mistress for fifteen years by whom he had a son. He was only too well aware of the fact that his sinfulness gravely affected his mother. "I have no words," he would later write, "to express the love she had for me, and how much more anguish she was now suffering the pangs of child-birth for my spiritual state than when she had given birth to me physically. I just cannot see how she could have been healed if my death in sin had come to pierce the entrails of her love."

Those early years of unbridled sensuality revealed him to be a man of innate passion—a character trait that would continue to dominate the rest his life. Even after he committed himself to a chaste and virtuous Christian life, his natural vitality, vibrancy, and verve was evident. But those early years also uniquely bonded moth-er and son in a way that would shape the rest of their lives—she in committed intercession, he in continued gratitude.

In pursuit of opportunities to improve his academic standing he took teaching posts—opportunities Monica secured for him first in Rome and later in Milan. It was in this latter city that he fell under the sway of the eloquent bishop and rhetorician Ambrose. After a long and tortured battle of the soul, Augustine was converted to orthodox Christianity under Ambrose's ministry and was baptized—much to the ecstatic relief of Monica.

After some two years of intensive discipling and catechizing, he returned to Africa and established a scholastic community in Hippo. There he founded a *Classicum Academae*—a kind of prototype for the modern university devoted to study, writing, and the work of cultural transformation. The school was famed for its emphasis on logic, rhetoric, art, music, politics, theology, and philosophy. But it was equally recognized for the brilliance of its founder.

In 391 the steadfastness, holiness, and giftedness of Augustine was recognized and he was ordained—though very much against his own objections. In 394 he was asked to serve as coadjutor in the diocese. And in 396 he was elevated to the bishopric of the city.

During his career he wrote more than a thousand works, including nearly three hundred hefty books. Amazingly, these writings have endured the test of time. Indeed, several of them have claimed a central place in the canon of the Western literary classics. His autobiography, *Confessions*, practically invented the genre and remains a devotional and inspirational classic. His commentaries on

Genesis and Psalms are of inestimable value to theologians and ecclesiastical scholars. His apologetic works *Contra Manichae* or *Contra Pelagae* continue to set the standard for the defense of Biblical orthodoxy. His didactae like *Sanctus Dei* or *De Trinitate* formed the first, and arguably among the best, systematic theologies the Western church has ever produced. And his pastoral works such as the *Enchiridion* served generations as a practical handbook for daily Christian living.

But he is probably best known for—and made his greatest contribution with—his analysis of the culture war here on earth and its relation to the war in the heavenlies. *The City of God* is a book that both summarizes his other works and crowns them with the full achievement of maturity. It is a combative book—like so much of his writing, it confronts the intellectual and spiritual errors that inevitably crop up both within and without the church. The reason that he devoted so much of the work—and indeed why he spent so much of his life and work—critiquing the pagan philosophies of the world and exposing the aberrant theologies of the church was that Augustine believed that those things matter not only in the realm of eternity determining the spiritual destiny of masses of humanity but in the realm of the here and now determining the temporal destiny of whole civilizations.

Perhaps it was precisely because Augustine was not an ivory tower academic that he was able to make such a clear connection between his faith and his practice—between orthodoxy and orthopraxy. He lived his entire life in the midst of a vibrant community and among enduring friends and disciples. Augustine was a social being. He loved the company of others. They not only sharpened his thinking, they softened his heart.

But while he had many friends, the remarkable relationship he had forged over the years with his mother was far and away the most significant. After his conversion, he immediately sent for her. She ultimately helped him organize the little academic community that began to grow up around him in the countryside outside of Milan. She walked him though those early days of trial and temptation, doubt and depression. She became his most trusted confidante. And she provoked him to pursue the studies and the writing that would ultimately place him in the pantheon of greatness.

Following her brief final illness, Augustine was riven with sadness—not merely because he had lost his mother, but because also his dearest friend. Indeed, his faith could bear him up in under the specter of death, but there was little to console the loss of companionship. Thus, he wrote, "I closed her eyes; and there streamed withal a mighty sorrow into my heart, which was overflowing with tears; mine yeses at the same time, by a violent command of my mind, drank up their fountain wholly dry; and woe was me in such a strife. But when she breathed her last, Adeodatus burst out into a loud lament; then checked by us all, held his peace. In like manner also a childish feeling in me, which was, through my heart's youthful voice, finding its vent in weeping, was checked and silenced. For we thought it not fitting to solemnise that funeral with tearful lament and groans: for this can only be taken to express grief for the departed, as though they were unhappy or altogether dead; whereas she was neither unhappy in her death, nor altogether dead. Of this we were assured on good grounds, the testimony of her good conversation and her faith unfeigned. What then was it which did grievously pain me within, but a fresh wound wrought through the sudden wrench of that most sweet and dear friendship? I joyed in her testimony, when, in that her last sickness, mingling her endearments with my acts of duty, she called me 'dutiful,' and mentioned with great affection of love, that she never had heard any harsh or reproachful sound uttered by my mouth against her. But yet, oh my God, who madest us, what comparison is there betwixt that honor that I paid to her, and her compassionate sacrifices for me? Being then forsaken of so great a comfort in her, my soul was wounded, and that life rent asunder as it were, which, of hers and mine together in friendship, had been made but one."

According to biographer Peter Brown, "Few mothers can survive being presented to us exclusively in terms of what they have come to mean to their sons, much less a son as complicated as Augustine." Nevertheless, Monica survives—indeed, she thrives. Theirs grew from a mere familial love into a genuine friendship—one that not only helped to shape who they were, but through the influence of Augustine, helped to shape Western civilization itself.

Kindness

*F*riendships are built upon the foundation of kindness. Common interests, shared backgrounds, coincident aspirations, and like minds go only so far in weaving the bonds of intimacy. More important than all these assumed attributes is an evident and demonstrable tenderheartedness. This is a fact that hardly escaped the attention of the great men and women of the past.

"We cannot tell the precise moment when friendship is formed. As in filling a vessel drop by drop, there is at last a drop which makes it run over; so in a series of kindnesses there is at last one which makes the heart run over."

James Boswell, 1740-1795

"How easy is it for one benevolent being to diffuse pleasure around him, and how truly is a kind heart a fountain of gladness, making everything in its vicinity to freshen into smiles."

Washington Irving, 1783-1859

Kind words produce their own image in men's souls;
and a beautiful image it is. They soothe and quiet and
comfort the hearer. They shame him out of his sour,
morose, unkind feelings. We have not yet begun to
use kind words in such abundance as they ought to be
used."

Blaise Pascal, 1623-1662

"The ministry of kindness is a treasured aspect of
friendship which may be inherited by all men, rich
and poor, learned and illiterate. Brilliance of mind
and capacity for deep thinking have rendered great
service to humanity, but by themselves they are impo-
tent to dry a tear or mend a broken heart."

Leonardo da Vinci, 1452-1519

If I can stop one heart from breaking
I shall not live in vain:
If I can ease one life in the aching,
Or cool one pain,
Or help one fainting robin
Unto his nest again,
I shall not live in vain.

Emily Dickenson, 1830-1886

"The balm of life, a kind and faithful friend."

Arthur Quiller-Couch, 1863-1944

"Friendship may begin in a shared passion and be carried along by a shared interest, but in the end it must suffer if not bolstered, nurtured, and sustained by the stronger implements of tender affection and gracious sympathy. A friend is he who has shared mutual ministrations of kindness."

Charlotte Bronte, 1816-1855

"Always, sir, set a high value on spontaneous kindness. He whose inclination prompts him to cultivate your friendship of his own accord, will love you more than one whom you have been at pains to attach to."

Samuel Johnson, 1709-1784

"There is a sort of great man who makes his friends feel small. But the authentic great man makes his friends feel great."

G.K. Chesterton, 1874-1936

"Let your hand feel for the afflictions and distresses of everyone, and let your hand give in proportion to your purse; remembering always the estimation of the widows mite, that it is not everyone that asketh that deserveth charity; all however are worthy of the inquiry, or the deserving may suffer. Thus is the mettle of true character."

George Washington, 1732-1799

Kindly affections,
And gentle ministrations,
Hallowed intimacies,
And generous sympathies:
Such are the appliances
Of trust;
Such are the devices
Of friendship.

Tristan Gylberd, 1954-

"It is easier to forgive an enemy than to forgive a friend. Surely, this ought not ever be the accepted case save in those rarest of all cases and upon the direst of all occasions when no other honorable resolution condescends to make its manifest appearance straightway."

William Blake, 1757-1827

What is the greatest of all the virtues?
Perhaps order, if we were but citizens,
Or knowledge, if we were but students,
Or pleasure, if we were but fools,
Or beauty, if we were but lovers,
Or freedom, if we were but insurgents,
Or fame, if we were but egotists.
But the greatest of all the virtues,
Surely is kindness, if we were but friends.

Robert Hunter, 1823-1897

"Kind words bring no blisters on the tongue that speaks them nor on the ear which hears them. Kind words are never wasted. Like scattered seeds, they spring up in unexpected places. Kindness is a conquering weapon. Kindness should not be all on one side. One good turn must have another as its return, or it will not be fair. He who expects kindness should show kindness. This is the high and holy mark of friendship."

Charles Haddon Spurgeon, 1834-1892

"Treat your friends as you do your pictures; place them in their best light."

Auguste Renior, 1841-1919

The quality of mercy is not strained;
It droppeth as the gentle rain from Heaven
Upon the palce beneath; it is twice blest:
It blesseth him that gives and him that takes:
Tis the mightiest in the mightiest, it becomes
The throned monarch better than his crown:
His scepter shows the force of temporal power,
The attribute to awe and majesty,
Wherein doth sit the dread and fear of kings;
But mercy is above this sceptered sway:
It is enthroned in the hearts of kings,
It is an attribute to God Himself;
And earthly power doth then show likest God's
When mercy seasons justice.

William Shakespeare, c. 1564-1616

GEORGE WASHINGTON, 1732-1799
AND THOMAS MIFFLIN, 1744-1800

According to the majority of eighteenth and nineteenth century historians, the most remarkable event during America's Founding Era did not take place on a battlefield. It did not occur during the course of the constitutional debates. It was not recorded during the great diplomatic negotiations with France, Spain, or Holland. It did not take place at sea, or in the assemblies of the states, or in the counsels of war. It was instead when the field commander of the continental armies surrendered his commission to the congressional authorities at Annapolis.

It was when General George Washington, the victorious conqueror of the greatest military power on the face of the earth, resigned his officer's commission.

At the time, he was the idol of the country and his soldiers. Due to the decrepitude of the national treasury the army was unpaid, and the veteran troops, well armed and fresh from their stunning success at Yorktown, were eager to have him take control of the seemingly disordered country. Some wanted to crown him king. Others thought to make him a dictator or protector—rather like the great Parliamentary reformer, Oliver Cromwell, had been a century earlier in England.

With the loyal support of the army and the enthusiasm of the populous, it would have been easy enough for Washington to have made himself the ruler of the new nation. But instead, he did the unthinkable. He resigned. And like the great Roman predecessor, Cincinnatus, he returned to the plow. He simply appeared before President Thomas Mifflin and his cabinet and submitted himself to their governance and then came home to his beloved Mount Vernon as an ordinary citizen.

According to historian Henry Cabot Lodge, what he said on that remarkable occasion was "one of the two most memorable speeches ever made in the United States." Thus it was on December 23, 1783 that the general said: "Mr. President, the great events on which my resignation depended having at length taken place, I have now the honor of offering my sincere congratulations to Congress, and of presenting myself before them, to surrender into their hands the trust committed to me and to claim the indulgence of retiring from the service of my country. Happy in the confirmation of our independence and sovereignty, and pleased with the opportunity afforded the United States of becoming a respectable nation, I resign with satisfaction the appointment I accepted with diffidence. The successful termination of the war has verified the most sanguine expectations, and my gratitude for the interposition of Providence and the assistance I have received from my countrymen increases with every review of the momentous contest. I consider it an indispensable duty to close this last solemn act of my official life by commending the interests of our dearest country to the protection of Almighty God, and those who have the superintendence of them to His holy keeping. Having now finished the work assigned me, I retire from the great theater of action, and, bidding an affectionate farewell to this august body, under whose orders I have so long acted, I here offer my commission and take my leave of all the employments of public life."

Writing of this remarkable scene, Henry Wadsworth Longfellow exclaimed: "Which was the most splendid spectacle ever witnessed—the opening feast of Prince George in London, or the resignation of Washington? Which is the noble character for after-ages to admire—yon fribble dancing in lace and spangles, or yon hero who

sheathes his sword after a life of spotless honor, a purity unre-
proached, a courage indomitable, and a consummate victory?"

The answer to most Americans was obvious: Washington was
"first in war, first in peace, and first in the hearts of his countrymen."

Though he had often wrangled in disagreement with his superi-
ors over matters of military strategy, pay schedules, supply ship-
ments, troop deployment, and the overlap of civil and martial
responsibilities, there was never any question of his ultimate loyalty
or allegiance. In the end, he always submitted himself to the authority God had placed over him.

And that was no mean feat.

Washington had faithfully served under eleven different
American presidents at a time of severest crisis. The first two held
office prior to the signing of the Declaration of Independence—
Peyton Randolph of Virginia and Henry Middleton of South
Carolina. The next six held office between the time of the
Declaration and the ratification of the first confederated constitu-
tion—John Hancock of Massachusetts, Henry Laurens of South
Carolina, John Jay of New York, Samuel Huntington of

Connecticut, Samuel Johnson of North Carolina, and Thomas
McKean of Delaware. The last three held office under the Articles
of Confederation—John Hanson of Maryland, Elias Budinot of New
Jersey, and finally, Thomas Mifflin of Pennsylvania. Another four
presidents would hold office during Washington's short interlude
away from public life prior to the ratification of the current constitution—Richard Henry Lee of Virginia, Nathaniel Gorham of
Massachusetts, Arthur St. Clair of Pennsylvania, and Cyrus Griffin
of Virginia. During all those trying days, under each of those varied
men, General Washington gave himself whole-heartedly to the loyal
task of selfless service.

He obeyed orders. He rendered due respect. He yielded to the
authority of lawful office and jurisdiction. He met the sundry needs
of the hour. He set aside personal ambition, personal preference,
personal security, and at times, personal opinion in order to serve.

Of this remarkable posture before God and men, Lodge wrote:
"Few men in all time have such a record of achievement. Still fewer
can show at the end of a career so crowded with high deeds and
memorable victories a life so free from spot, a character so unselfish
and pure."

"His true greatness was evidenced," said the pundit Henry Adams, "in the fact that he never sought greatness, but rather service." The dean of American historians, Francis Parkman concurred that it was this "remarkable spirit of the servant" that ultimately "elevated him even higher in his countrymen's estimations than he already was." And biographer Paul Butterfield, wrote, "He never countenanced the sin of omission when it came to duty to God or country. His was a life of constant service in the face of mankind's gravest need." Thus, historian John Richard Green commented, "no nobler figure ever stood in the forefront of a country's life. Never did he shrink from meeting the need of the hour. He was our national guardian."

George Washington lived a life of service. He practiced what we today call servant-leadership. He would settle for nothing less. He would strive for nothing more. And he left the disposition of the matter of his life and fortune in the hands of God.

Interestingly, this posture of service was made felicitously easier on the occasion of his resignation by the fact that Thomas Mifflin was his most faithful advocate. By an ironic sort of providence, Mifflin served as Washington's first aide-de-camp at the beginning of the Revolutionary War, and, when the war was over, he was the man, as President of the fledgling republic, who accepted Washington's resignation of his commission.

In the years between, Mifflin not only served the cause of freedom as the first Quartermaster General of the Continental Army he also served as Washington's dearest friend, greatest political ally, and most trusted confidante.

He had been responsible for obtaining desperately needed supplies for the troops—and though he was at times suspected of making excessive profit himself, he had an uncanny knack for such procurement and was credited with many of the army's earliest successes. Although experienced in business and proficient in obtaining supplies for the war, Mifflin actually preferred the front lines, and he distinguished himself in military actions on Long Island and near Philadelphia. It was there that Washington gained a deep respect and a warm regard for his friend. He was encouraged by the younger man's ingenuity. He was reassured by his passion. He was comforted by his allegiance. And he was revitalized by his commitment. That commitment had cost him dearly though—born and reared a Quaker, Mifflin was excluded from their meetings for his military activities.

Their relationship—as is the case with most foxhole friendships—was not without its conflicts. A controversial figure, Mifflin
lost favor with Washington for a time when he joined the so-called
Conway Cabal—a desperate plan during an especially difficult peri-
od in the war to replace Washington as Commander-in-Chief of the
Continental Army with rival General Horatio Gates. Washington
had yet to win a single engagement and the military prospects of the
young country had become rather grim. Later, Mifflin narrowly
missed court-martial action over his handling of funds by resigning
his commission in 1778.

In spite of these problems—and of repeated charges that he was a
drunkard—Mifflin continued to be elected to positions of responsibility—as President and Governor of Pennsylvania, delegate to the
Constitutional Convention, as well as the highest office in the land.
In addition, he continued to be Washington's friend. Indeed, during
the tenure of his presidential administration—he served from
November 3, 1783 to November 29, 1784—he was Washington's
strongest supporter in the national government. And the fact that it
was his hand on the tiller of the ship of state that gave the general

confidence that he could resign in good conscience and with full assurance.

Though most of Mifflin's greatest contributions occurred in his earlier years—as Governor of Pennsylvania, he supported improvements of roads, and reformed the State penal and judicial systems, in the First and Second Continental Congresses he was firm in his stand for independence, in his administration he signed the treaty that guaranteed that independence, at the Constitutional Convention he helped to forge the document that established that independence—it was that final symbolic gesture that enshrines his name in the annals of American history.

It was a friendship that served as the backdrop to America's most poignant scene of selfless service. America's peculiar experiment in liberty and freedom was given life because of the covenantal bonds forged by two strong men—men who trusted each other because they knew each other well.

· BEST FRIENDS ·

Remembrance

Friends always have a lingering, lasting effect on us. Their kindnesses remain with us long after they have departed. Their example still inspires us. Their words continue to impact our thinking. They intrude upon our daily concourse with a gentle but certain regularity. Remembrance has thus always been an essential element of the friendships of great men and women, a kind of eternal trophy of a gracious endowment.

Were a star quenched on high,
   For Ages would its light,
Still travelling downward from the sky,
   Shine on our mortal sight.
So when a great man dies,
   For years beyond our ken,
The light he leaves behind him lies
   Upon the paths of men.

Henry Wadsworth Longfellow, 1807-1882

"Thinking of departed friends is to me something
sweet and mellow. For when I had them with me it
was with the feeling that I was going to lose them,
and now that I have lost them I keep the feeling that I
have them with me still."

Abraham Kuyper, 1837-1920

Of a time, there comes for all of us a poignant moment—a moment when we search for our ultimate calling and destiny. It is there and then that we see ourselves in the speculum of our lives—an ethereal presence staring back at us, a reminder of our place in the world. But it is not the reflection which confirms our purpose. If we need only see ourselves to be affirmed, we would all be bound by the ties of narcissism, needing only a house of mirrors to comfort us. It is the vision of image upon image that establishes just who we are and what we are to do—it is seeing ourselves in the context of community, of relationships, and of friendships that ultimately gives meaning to our search for meaning and purpose in life. Indeed, no man is an island.

Andrew Nelson Lytle, 1905-1996

Should auld acquaintance be forgot
And never brought to mind?
Should auld acquaintance be forgot
And days o' lang syne?

For auld lang syne, my dear
For auld lang syne
We'll tak' a cup o' kindness yet
For auld lang syne?

We twa ha'e run about the braes
And pu't the gowans fine
But we've wandered mony a weary foot
Sin'auld lang syne.

For auld lang syne, my dear
For auld lang syne
We'll tak' a cup o' kindness yet
For auld lang syne?

We twa ha'e paidl't i' the burn
Frae mornin' sun till dine
But seas between us braid ha'e roared
Sin auld lang syne.

For auld lang syne, my dear
For auld lang syne
We'll tak' a cup o' kindness yet
For auld lang syne?

And here's a hand, my trustie fiere
And gie's a hand o' thine
And we'll tak' a right guid willie waught
For auld lang syne.

For auld lang syne, my dear
For auld lang syne
We'll tak' a cup o' kindness yet
For auld lang syne?

And surely ye'll be your pint-stoup
And surely I'll be mine
And we'll tak' a cup o' kindness yet
For auld lang syne.

Robert Burns, 1759-1796

"He being dead yet speaketh."

Paul of Tarsus, c.10-65

"I need my friends more and more, and the great world grows wider, and dear ones fewer—I miss my biggest heart; my own goes wandering round and calls out. Friends are too dear to sunder, O they are far too few, and how soon they will go away where we cannot find them. Don't let us forget these things, for their remembrance now will save us many an anguish when it is too late to love them."

Emily Dickinson, 1830-1886

Brother Bryan, 1863-1941
and Leslie Kettering, 1919-1994

Birmingham, Alabama was a wild and untamed mining town in the heart of the reconstructed South when James Alexander Bryan came to pastor the Third Presbyterian Church there in 1888. When he died in 1941, Birmingham had become a vibrant industrial center. In the years between, Brother Bryan—as he was affectionately called—won the hearts of generation after generation of her citizens.

He was an unlikely hero for the bustling town, though. For one thing, he was noticeably inept as a pulpiteer. His sermons were often halting, rambling, and inarticulate. Though entirely committed to the authority of the Scriptures and the centrality of preaching, he simply was not a skilled orator.

He was also a poor administrator. He was notoriously disorganized. When it came to the niggling details of management, he was often absent-minded and forgetful. He never seemed to lose sight of the "big picture," but all the necessary increments just got lost in the shuffle. Though perpetually busy, he was easily distracted and rarely kept up with his workload.

He didn't even maintain a particularly winsome appearance. He was more often than not disheveled, shabbily dressed, and hastily groomed. He was shy, soft-spoken, and had a slight stutter. In a day and time when manliness and imposing presence was especially esteemed, he was merely slight and retiring.

Not surprisingly, during his long tenure as pastor, his church never really grew. When he died, membership stood at just under a hundred—right where it was shortly after he arrived in Birmingham a half-century earlier.

Nevertheless, he was practically a cultural icon in the city. Near the end of his life of service, he was honored by local leaders and dignitaries in a city-wide celebration. The president of the City Commission said: "No man in Birmingham is better known or better loved than Brother Bryan. There is one man in this city about whom we are all agreed, and he is Brother Bryan." The editor of the city newspaper agreed: "Brother Bryan is the only man, whom we have ever known, whose motives have never been questioned. He is the one man for whom we are all unanimous."

The city erected a statue of the humble pastor at one of her busiest intersections near downtown. It portrayed him in a posture of prayer and proclaimed him "the patron saint of Birmingham." On

the occasion of its unveiling, Hugo Black, the United States Supreme
Court Justice, asserted: "This dedication raises our community to its
loftiest heights, just as Brother Bryan has all these long years of his
faithful and selfless service. The statue, let us hope, will inspire those
here today, those who know Brother Bryan, and all those who come
after, to love our neighbors as ourselves, even as he has."

When Brother Bryan died, the entire city mourned his passing.
Thousands of men, women, and children from every walk of life
crowded around the tiny sanctuary and followed the solemn cortege
at his funeral. Flags were lowered to half-mast and the mayor proclaimed an official day of prayer and fasting.

How had this seemingly inept pastor won over an entire city so
completely? How had this painfully ordinary man accomplished a
feat so extraordinary as this?

Very simply, Brother Bryan was a common man who proved to
be an uncommon example of the Christian mandate of "doing justice, loving mercy, and walking humbly before God." Though he
violated all the rules of success, church growth, worldly acclaim, and
effectiveness, he seemed to incarnate the essence of the faith once
and for all delivered unto the saints. He was, as many called him,
"religion in shoes."

He made it a habit to make a circuit every morning just before dawn to all the factories, shops, fire and police stations, schools, and offices downtown to pray with as many common working men and women as he could. He would simply announce himself, drop to his knees wherever he was, and begin to intercede for each of them. Over time, his obvious piety became a cherished emblem of personal concern in a harshly impersonal industrial world. He was the unofficial chaplain to the entire community—it was often said that the words most often on his lips were, "Let us pray."

Brother Bryan also distinguished himself with his selfless service to the poor, the needy, the brokenhearted, and the sick. His indefatigable efforts to encourage the distressed led him to establish several city outreaches to the homeless, to orphans and widows, and to the victims of war and pestilence overseas. More than any rich philanthropist, more than any well-endowed foundation, more than any charitable institution, he demonstrated the power and effect of merciful service on the fabric of a community.

Though a confirmed non-partisan politically, he often lobbied magistrates when issues of justice arose—he was, for instance, an early champion of civil rights and racial reconciliation. His unassailable character, his pure motives, and his holy demeanor enabled him to take such controversial stands without polarizing or alienating his beloved fellow citizens. Somehow they seemed to understand that his commitment to justice was a natural outgrowth of his humble faith and merciful service—the one could not be had without the others.

When he was already an elderly man—eleven years past the normal retirement age—when he first met the young Leslie Kettering. She was a victim of the Great Depression—still fiercely ravaging the deep South as late as 1938. Abandoned by her impoverished parents when she was just sixteen, she had made her way from the sharecropping Tennessee River valley to the city. There she quickly fell into a desperate life of petty crime and prostitution.

Though he was practically an invalid by then, Brother Bryan still made his prayer rounds in those days. Early one morning he discovered Leslie cowering in an alley, where she had spent the previous night. He immediately took her home and tended to her wounds—both internal and external.

The Bryan household had "adopted" many waifs, orphans, vagabonds, and urchins through the years. But with Leslie, what began as a not uncommon mission of mercy ended as a remarkable friendship. Following an extraordinary conversion, this very unlikely candidate for the work of the ministry became what Brother

Bryan called "my very right arm." She stayed in the Bryan home for the next three years—serving the venerable old man as a daughter, secretary, nurse, counselor, prayer partner, and friend.

In his final years, she helped him with his burgeoning correspondence, with his frequent radio broadcasts, and with his pastoral tasks. But more, she became a kind of intimate emblem of everything that his life and work had stood for. She was, as he often remarked, "a trophy of grace." She who had been utterly friendless was not only befriended, but she had herself befriended—and thus had become a great consolation to one of the most remarkable men of a now practically forgotten old world order.

On the day following his funeral, the newspaper in Birmingham commented: "We have had set before us the clearest example of what it must mean to be a follower of Christ. There can be little doubt to anyone familiar with Brother Bryan's life and work that the high ideals of the faith may actually be manifested. And that poses a tremendously prophetic challenge to us all."

For the rest of her long life—a life devoted to service akin to that of her great friend, on the mission field in southern India among the despised "untouchable" castes—Leslie Kettering would happily affirm the truth of that statement. Her friendship with Brother

Bryan not only changed her life, her destiny, and her impact on the world, it changed his.

"Do you remember the first time we met? Of course, first impressions are important only in light of what history, experience, or revelation may tell us. Your friendship taught me that."

Andy Tant, 1980-1996